Black Helicopters Over America
Strikeforce for the New World Order

Black Helicopters Over America

Strikeforce for the New World Order

Jim Keith

1994
IllumiNet Press

Library of Congress Cataloging in Publication Data

Keith, Jim, 1949—
    Black Helicopters Over America : Strikeforce for the New World Order /
Jim Keith
        p.   cm.
    ISBN: 1-881532-05-4 : $12.95
    1.   United States — Politics and government — 1989-
    2.   Conspiracies — United States — History — 20th Century.
    3.   Democracy — United States.
    4.   World politics — 1989-   I. Title
E839.5.K45   1994
322.4'2'0973—dc20   94-23888

IllumiNet Press
P.O. Box 2808
Lilburn, Georgia 30226

Cover design by Margaret Rhodes, Christopher Street and Jeffrey Stoner

10 9 8 7 6 5

Printed in the United States of America

Dedicated to those who resist the New World Order

I would like to thank the following people for their assistance during the writing of this book: Linda Tierney, Ron Bonds, Sam Rountree and Jerry Elwood Smith. I am particularly indebted to Robert Sonderfan for his excellent research assistance, and to Thomas Adams, whose painstaking documentation of the black choppers was utilized extensively in this book.

The author is always interested in hearing from individuals who have information about world conspiracy. I may be contacted care of IllumiNet Press. Enclose a SASE if you would like a reply.

Table of Contents

On Militarism

"There isn't a trick in the racketeering bag that the military gang is blind to. It has its 'finger men' to point out enemies, its 'muscle men' to destroy enemies, its 'brain guys' to plan war preparations, and a 'Big Boss,' Supra-nationalistic Capitalism.

"It may seem odd for me a military man, to adopt such a comparison. Truthfulness compels me to do so. I spent thirty five years and four months in active service as a member of our country's most agile military force, the Marine Corps. I served in all commissioned ranks from 2nd Lieutenant to Major General. During that period I spent most of my life being a high class muscle man for big business, for Wall Street, and for the Bankers. In short I was a racketeer — a gangster for Capitalism.

"I suspected I was just part of the racket at the time. Now I am sure of it. Like all members of the military profession I never had an original thought until I left the Service. My mental faculties remained in suspended animation, while I obeyed the orders of the higher-ups. This is typical with everyone in the military.

"Thus I helped to make Mexico, and especially Tampico, safe for American oil interests in 1914. I helped to make Haiti and Cuba a decent place for the National City Bank Boys to collect revenue. I helped in the raping of half a dozen Central American Republics for the benefit of Wall Street. The record of racketeering is long. I helped purify Nicaragua for the International Banking House of Brown Brothers in 1909-1912. I brought light to the Dominican Republic for American sugar interests in 1916. In China in 1927 I helped Standard Oil.

"During those years I had, as the boys in the back room would say, a swell racket. I was rewarded with honors, medals, and promotion. Looking back on it, I feel that I might have given Al Capone a few hints. The best he could do was operate in three city districts. I operated on three continents."

— Major-General Smedley Butler, USMC, quoted in *Money,* December, 1951.

Preface

Klamath Falls, Oregon (API). Another important step forward in the disarming of America took place in a city in Oregon yesterday. Klamath Falls, located in the southern Cascade Mountains, is Oregon's fifth largest population center and home to Kingsley Field, the state's only Air Force Base. This was the latest city to be chosen for an all-out assault on criminal gun owners.

The military operation held yesterday was a large-scale effort to take the guns out of the hands of the criminals and to "Turn the screws hard on the lawless element in our society" as the Attorney General stated earlier in the week. While the details of what took place are still somewhat sketchy, officials are declaring that the operation was a total success, with few fatalities and a minimum of property damage reported.

At 5:00 a.m. on Tuesday, approximately three dozen unmarked, black helicopters appeared on the horizon of Klamath Falls in a surprise raid on the lawbreakers. Armored personnel carriers, tanks and supply trucks simultaneously descended upon the city from the highways. Tanks and armored vehicles were used to set up checkpoints on all of the major thoroughfares leading into or out of the area, and were employed in assaults on several reported hot spots of resistance.

At 5:39 a.m. radio and television broadcasts were replaced with pre-taped programs which repeated the following message:

"This is your government keeping you informed for your own protection. The community of Klamath Falls is cooperating in a scheduled search operation for illegal weaponry, as authorized by version 3-B, section 522 of the Brady Bill. Be assured that these are completely legal measures which are being taken, and law-abiding citizens have nothing to fear. Repeat. Law abiding citizens have nothing to fear. During the next few hours black helicopters will be hovering over neighborhoods in your town, using advanced electronic scanners to determine violations of Section 587, dealing with the criminal possession of guns. Homes which are found to be in compliance with the statute will be passed over, and the occupants may go about their business. Any dwelling found to be containing firearms will be secured by members of the National Police Force and all firearms will be confiscated. All inhabitants of the dwelling where firearms are found will be considered to be in direct violation of Section 587 and will be placed under immediate arrest by the authorities.

"Do not be alarmed by this routine check. Members of urban youth groups have been temporarily drafted to aid in the seizure of firearms. These black-uniformed units will be entering homes determined to be in violation by the helicopter scanning.

"All citizens are to remain in their homes until the scheduled search is completed. Citizens have until 10:00 a.m. to place any overlooked weapons which they have not yet turned in on their doorsteps. This illegal weaponry will be picked up by the National Police Force and will not appear as a violation of Act 587. When this scheduled search and seizure operation is completed, you will be notified by announcements on radio and television.

"We must all be protected from the real criminals who hide weapons in order to use them later in the commission of crimes against innocent victims. Finally measures are being taken to restore law and order to our communities in this great land of ours. Have a peaceful and law-abiding day."

This message was repeated throughout the day. Helicopter scanning began at precisely 10:00 a.m. Hundreds of automatic and semi-automatic rifles and handguns appeared on doorsteps throughout Klamath Falls as the National Police Force and armed urban units proceeded house-to-house, collecting the weapons and placing them in waiting trucks.

At 11:27 a.m. the first violation was noted at the dwelling of Jay Driessler, a person well known in the community for his subversive views and membership in several groups which authorities have characterized as "hate groups" and "neo-Nazi." Driesslers's dwelling was quickly secured by the National Police Force. After shots were heard from within the house, tear gas was fired and the house was forcibly entered. Driessler, resisting arrest by the authorities, was the only casualty in the incident. Driessler's house was accidentally burned down, reportedly due to a weapons misfire hitting a gas main.

At 12:03 p.m. another violent confrontation took place near the center of town. A routine helicopter scan showed 137 alleged cult members of the right-wing United Church illegally congregated in a cult-owned building located on East Main Street. The head of the cult was Rick Armstrong, a person well-known in the area for his extremist religious views and radio broadcasts warning of the "Last Days" and the "Mark of the Beast."

By 1:15 p.m. the cult compound was surrounded by approximately 200 members of the National Police Force. All four entrances to the building were breached simultaneously and the cult members were taken into custody. There were only five fatalities in the raid: Rick Armstrong, the cult leader; Charlene Armstrong, his wife; and three of Armstrong's lieutenants, who attempted to resist arrest. Remaining cult members were marched 1 and 1/2 miles to awaiting trucks, where they were taken to a detainment center in nearby Tulelake, California for further processing.

Gunfire was heard at several other locations in the city during the course of the day, but so far we have no information on these incidents.

At a press conference held this afternoon, reporters were shown a near mountain of contraband weapons confiscated during the Klamath Falls anti-guns operation. These included many varieties of auto- and semiautomatic weapons as well as more exotic military weapons, including surface-to-air missiles and hand grenades alleged to have been hidden in the basement of the Armstrong cult compound.

While authorities would not further elaborate from whom these weapons had been confiscated pending court trials of the individuals involved, they did indicate that at least two armed encampments outside of town, similar to the infamous Mount Carmel compound of the Branch Davidians of Waco, Texas, had been stormed and secured by government forces. The criminals apprehended in these raids were described to reporters as dangerous gun hoarders, arms dealers, armed insurrectionists, and offbeat cultists. Officials indicated that over 300 such undesirables had been captured and were now being detained in facilities set up at the local National Guard armory, at Kingsley Field, and in Tulelake, California. Wing Commander John Theoharis, in charge of the fighter helicopter squadron assigned to Kingsley Field was accidentally killed in a weapons-related mishap at the base. According to official sources, this occurred in the early minutes of the anti-guns operation, during what was an otherwise calm transfer of authority from local officials to federal authorities.

Life for the average citizen of Klamath Falls, Oregon appears to continue undisturbed the day following the National Police Force operation. Local newspaper and network affiliate TV stations experienced no disruption of service other than the public service broadcast which took place Tuesday. Authorities are dismissing as hysteria tales of radio stations being taken off the air and businesses being shut down. API has learned, however, that the FCC did suspend the license of one AM talk radio station for "not broadcasting in the interests of the public."

Becky Gross, spokeswoman for the U.S. West Telephone Company issued a statement that the service outages to the Klamath Falls area were entirely due to workmen cutting a fiber optic cable and were in no way connected to any sort of blackout or cover-up of events in the region, and apologized for the problem.

A press release from the White House late today urged all Americans to remain calm and to cooperate fully with authorities.

"This is a great day for America," the President said. "Safety and security is now at hand for all Americans. While taking away the guns will not totally put an end to crime, it will take firepower out of the hands of ordinary criminals, away from the lunatics and paranoids, and return it to our strong hands, giving us the power we need... to keep you safe."

If you are wondering, the above press release is wholly fictitious, and only written to illustrate a serious point. Call it the *War of the Worlds* radio broadcast, sans the little green men. The scenario which I have invented, however, reflects a possibility which is only too real, and that is a totalitarian takeover of the United States by our own government, beginning with a confiscation of our guns.

I would caution you not to laugh off the possibility of this latter-day 1984 taking place in America. There are more than enough warning signs that suggest that what you have just read is more than a fictional possibility. Those signs are all around us, for those who have the courage to look. And one of those alarming signs is the appearance of the black helicopters in the skies of America.

1

A Black Chopper Chronology 1971-1994

Unmarked black helicopters are flying over our land in violation of all local and federal laws, carrying on their secret business, and taunting and terrifying the populace. During the latter half of 1994 alone, hundreds of reports from all over the land of these ominous black craft have been circulating by word-of-mouth, via small "underground" and "patriot" newspapers, and on special interest computer bulletin boards, although very few of such sightings are reported by the mainstream newspapers or radio and television. These are not easily-dismissed occurrences linked to the lunatic fringe, but are often solid reports sometimes backed up by photos which cannot be disputed. Whatever powers are dispatching the black helicopters, however, this is not a new phenomenon. It is only the frequency of the black chopper sightings which have increased within the past few years. The following chronology is a year-by-year listing of significant sightings (but not all sightings that I have been able to accumulate) of black and unmarked mystery helicopters, and events associated with these occurrences:

1971

— We are able to first document sightings of the black helicopters beginning in August of 1971, in Lake County, Colorado. Forty sheep were found dead and "blistered" in some unknown manner, after a rancher observed a helicopter flying over the animals. This sighting was to set the pace for incidents to follow during this period of time, mystery chopper sightings often being linked to cattle rustling or cattle mutilation.

1973

— In April and May of 1973 there were at least four sightings of unmarked helicopters in Wayne County, Davis County, Audubon County, and Henry County in Iowa.

— In August of 1973 there were at least three separate sightings of choppers without identifying markings which took place in Illinois. In Missouri during the same month there were 41 sightings of unmarked helicopters which people found unusual enough to report to the Pike County Sheriff's Department.

— In September of 1973, in St. Francois County, Missouri, a man observed what he thought was a military helicopter, marked only by a large white spot on its tail section. In St. Louis County, in Missouri, James Hagler spotted a helicopter hovering over his property on three occasions. Hagler said that someone in the chopper fired on him the third time that it appeared, and that he fired shots back, only to be fired at again by someone on the ground. After a search by the police was completed, Hagler was fired at again.

— In Summer of 1973, in Jersey County, Illinois, a large unmarked white cargo helicopter was observed by Mrs. Phyliss Beutell and her son as the craft took off from a nearby field which contained a herd of cattle. During the same period of time unmarked helicopters were observed by several witnesses in Minnesota, while low-flying mystery helicopters were seen throughout the summer months by several witnesses in Kansas, events which immediately preceded a wave of cattle mutilations in the area.

Also in Summer of 1973, a deputy in Perry County, Missouri, spotted an unmarked helicopter flying over a ranch located near St. Mary's. At about the same time two deputies observed unmarked helicopters hovering over cattle on a ranch in St. Francois County.

1974

— In Pottawattamie County, Iowa, during July of 1974, a farmer, Robert Smith, was shot at from a black twin-engine airplane and a white helicopter. There were sightings reported of both the airplane and chopper flying in the locale "all Spring."

— In Nebraska, from the 11th through the 17th of August, 1974, mysterious helicopters and lights were seen each night by a number of witnesses, according to the sheriff of Knox County.

— In September, October, and November of 1974 there were at least four sightings of mystery choppers in Nebraska, in Elgin, Holt, Madison, and Cedar Counties, with three of these sightings tentatively linked to cattle mutilations.

— In 1974 (no information on date), in Long Island, New York, unmarked black helicopters identified as Chinooks touched down on a public beach in the early morning. Men in black uniforms carrying M-16 rifles threatened a local police officer who confronted them and demanded to know what was going on. Smaller black helicopters were observed in the vicinity at the same time, hovering over the ocean. Later reports suggested that the Army was transporting a warhead when one chopper had mechanical trouble, although this story has not been confirmed. It also seems highly unlikely that this was the reason behind the event, given the fact that the Army would not be anxious to publicize such an incident.

1975

— On January 22nd, 1975 began a remarkable "flap" of unmarked helicopters (often equipped with bright spotlights) in Texas which would last for three months. The flap began when an unmarked chopper was observed circling an area where a possibly-mutilated cow had been found an hour earlier.

— In February, in Wood County, Texas, Mrs. A. D. Cruse heard a loud helicopter circling her house. A mutilated cow was found on the property the following morning. Also in February numerous unidentified choppers were seen in Smith, Gregg, Bosque, Coryell, Hamilton, Camp, Kaufman, and Hopkins Counties in Texas.

Monday, February 24th, 1975, proved to be a signal day for sightings of unidentified helicopters in Texas. In Camp County, law officers spoke with the occupants of a chopper which had landed. The two men claimed to be student pilots from Barksdale Air Force Base in Louisiana. On the same night, there were at least four sightings which took place in Kaufman and Henderson Counties, in Texas. On the same night in Kaufman County, police deputies Carl Hall and Alton Ashworth responded to separate reports of sightings of mystery choppers, both men arriving at different locations, only to see the craft fly away.

The following day, February 25th, in Bexar County, Texas, Stanley Jasic spotted a silver helicopter flying at the distance of 1/4 mile away. A dead, mutilated cow was later found in the area. That same night, there were three sightings of unidentified choppers in Kaufman County, Texas

A farmer in Smith County, Texas watched as an unmarked helicopter hovered over his property on February the 27th, while on March 1st, Horace McQueen, a reporter for a local television station, rode with a state trooper as they pursued a mysterious chopper for several miles.

— Thomas R. Adams in his book *The Choppers - and the Choppers,* which chronicles mystery helicopters and cattle mutilations, informs us that, "The reports of low-flying helicopters spotlighting cattle ended (apparently) in May [in Texas]. In response to citizen complaints, the Federal Aviation Administration conducted an investigation in July and August. The Air Force denied having any helicopter activity in the area and, according to the FAA: 'The Army was operating some helicopters in [the] area earlier this year, but without more definitive information on dates, times, etc., they cannot confirm any specific flights. They stated it is not their policy to fly at night with their lights off.'"

— During April, May, June, and July of 1975 unmarked mystery choppers were sighted in Marshall County, Kansas, and in at least three instances in Alamosa County, Colorado. Now that the Texas flap had ended, mystery helicopter sightings suddenly went wild in Colorado in May, 1975. Is it possible that a major operation involving black choppers moved its sphere of operations to Colorado because of too much publicity in Texas? It is impossible to say at this time.

On the 29th of May, in Elbert County, Colorado, a sighting of an unmarked chopper was linked to a cattle mutilation.

— Three girls on horseback were chased by a helicopter on July, 17th in El Paso County, Colorado, with a large number of chopper sightings taking place at the same time. Editor-publisher John Hines took a photo of a mystery chopper the same night as the horseback chase. This area was to be the center of a great deal of cattle mutilation activity during the year 1975.

On July 23rd in Elbert County, Colorado, Undersheriff Bill Waugh observed a silent helicopter through his binoculars. The same night a search was undertaken by the police for a mystery chopper which appeared and re-appeared in Teller County. Within recent weeks of these events there had been 40 incidents of cattle mutilation in Teller County.

On July 27th two girls out walking were chased by a helicopter in Elbert County, Colorado. The helicopter was photographed and identified as an "Army Bell Ranger."

— In August of 1975 there were 25 or more sightings of mystery choppers in several counties in Colorado. These sightings included an incident in which a rancher was chased by a helicopter near Franktown, in Douglas County on the 8th, and an incident which took place in early August, in which a youth driving a tractor was followed by an unidentified chopper to his farmhouse, with the chopper hovering for several minutes over the house.

On August 21st, an unidentified chopper was pursued by law enforcement agents in both Kimball County, Nebraska, and Logan County, Colorado. During the chase the helicopter paused to hover over a SAC missile silo near Bushnell, Nebraska.

Ed Sanders published a report on the above incident in *The Cattle Report* for March, 1977, titled "The Air Force and the Great Chase of Northern Colorado." Sanders reported:

"The night of Wednesday, August 21, 1975 provided an example of a possible deliberate deception maneuver by cattle mutilators near Logan County, Colorado. The incident involved possible decoy men disguised as Air Force officers who may have been used to confuse and to throw off course a concerted land and air chase of helicopters thought to be involved in the plague of cattle mutilations in Logan County and nearby counties. Logan County is located in northeast Colorado sugar beet, grain and cattle country. During that summer the helicopters had been flying by night over Logan County, and the cattle had been found mutilated in the morning. Sheriff's officers and even private groups (such as I-80 Control, a group of CBers) had been organizing to give chase to these phantom copters.

"Around 10 p.m. on Wednesday, August 21, a helicopter was reported heading into Logan County from the east, and Sheriff

Tex Graves and his staff took chase. In addition to some 17 ground units that ultimately took part in the chase, Sheriff Graves rented a private plane in which two sheriff's officers and a pilot rode. The night was clear and the aircraft could run without lights. During the night, a pickup truck containing two purported Air Force officers began to assist the chase, claiming to be receiving over the radio in the truck radar information from Warren Air Force Base in Cheyenne, Wyoming, located northwest of Logan County. (There are a number of Minuteman missile sites in Logan County under the control of Warren Air Force Base). The sheriff's vehicles on the ground were not equipped to pick up the Air Force frequencies so had to rely on the information relayed from the pickup with the Air Force men, who would relate the supposed location of the aircraft being chased as indicated by radar at the Air Force base.

"Only the next day, after the chase was long over, did reporters and sheriff's officers learn from Warren Air Force Base that they had no radar system that could have been used to track the copters. The only radar facilities they had, they said, were weather radar facilities. Sheriff Graves later referred to the alleged helpers as a 'pickup with Air Force jokers playing games.' During the chase, which spilled over into southern Nebraska, the putative Air Force men in the pickup kept announcing that 'radar' indicated that there was another aircraft flying near the chase plane at various times, but the officers and pilot, three men with glasses, never saw a thing, Sheriff Graves told the Greeley, Colorado, *Tribune*. The chase ended around 4:30 in the morning near a missile site in Southwest Nebraska, when the spotter plane lost sight of the phantom copter. The plane, reporter Bill Jackson of the Sterling, Colorado, *Journal-Advocate*, told us, 'saw the lights of the thing below them, and you know, it was a clear night. and when the light went out, that's what everybody thought, that they'd landed, but when the plane came down to 100-150 feet, he couldn't see anything... The only thing that was there was a missile silo.'

Several questions remain after this incident: (1) Were the two officers from the Air Force merely practical jokers having fun with local law enforcement? (It must be remembered that, in addition to Logan County officers, the Nebraska State Police and the Kimball County, Nebraska, sheriff's office were also involved.) (2) Were the two men merely masquerading as Air Force personnel & were they actually part of a mutilation network? (This network must have spent millions of dollars on copter fuel, maintenance, security and man-hours in the many states that have suffered mutilations) (3) Sad to ask is this: Is the United States Air Force involved in supplying cover for the mutilators?"

August of 1975 was also the beginning of a "Montana flap," and by May of 1976 there were at least 130 reports of helicopters and unidentified craft which had been observed in that state. During this period black choppers were seen over sensitive military installations, and these sightings occurred during the same period as similar over flights of military installations in Maine and Michigan.

— In September of 1975 there were over 40 sightings of unmarked choppers in Colorado, the incidents often occurring in areas where cattle mutilations were taking place.

In early September of 1975 a family in Rio Grande County, Colorado, observed a helicopter with something which looked like a "litter basket" hanging underneath it. The following day a mutilated bull was found nearby where the sighting had taken place, suggesting that the "litter basket" arrangement may have had something to do with the lifting or transporting of cattle.

On the 22nd of September, in Crowley and Pueblo Counties in Colorado, a man driving a pickup truck was forced off the road by a mystery chopper. He called for assistance on his CB and two policemen responded to the call. One policeman fired his rifle at the helicopter. Deputies from three counties, guards stationed at the Pueblo Army Depot, and Colorado State Police were led on a wild goose chase before the chopper finally eluded them. The helicopter made a sound "like the whistling of air coming from a tire." This report matches numerous chopper incidents in which witnesses say that these craft are quieter than regular helicopters, although they are not completely silent.

— October 1975 saw a continuance of the Colorado flap, with a minimum of 30 sightings being reported in the state.

On the 3rd of October in Weston County, Wyoming, Raymond "Spud" Jones and some of his neighbors woke up hearing a "high-pitched whine, like a jet turbine starting." On October 6th Jones found the mutilated carcass of one of his cows in a nearby pasture.

On October 7th Sheriff Willis Larson of Weston County, Wyoming, received a report that there was a helicopter hovering northeast of Newcastle. Larson drove to the site and observed the following, according to his report in the University of Wyoming's *Branding Iron* newspaper of October 14th:

"I reached the top of the ridge and saw an object to the west, near Highway 85 North," the sheriff said. "It was an orange, wedge-shaped object, resembling a helicopter in appearance. The tapered end had a bright red light. I was confused and looked at it through the binoculars," he said. "It was making sudden, jerky 'Z' movements, very fast, I thought. I called my wife and asked her to call Bockman to look at it." Bockman was already looking at the object, however. He reported it in the same position as the sheriff. The object descended and Larson lost sight of it. Bockman continued to observe it and saw it go down and its lights go out... "I called for a special deputy to take my position and dispatched another deputy to the south so we could bracket the object in a triangle," said the sheriff. "I then went to the airport. The mail plane was landing at the airport just as I arrived. Bockman pointed the object out to me. Thirty seconds later it went up and disappeared, just like shutting out a light. Later, as we were returning to town, a sudden bright flash lit the sky, like a flashbulb." An hour and a half later, the same lady [who had originally reported the chopper to Larson] called and reported the object in the same location. "I went out to check on it again, and the sky was split by five sudden flashes, in very quick succession, centered in the northeast," said the sheriff. Later a glowing light would appear in the eastern sky, and would be viewed by many residents. Lights rising over trees were reported by campers, brilliant flashes were reported by a motorist, and home owners saw strange lights. Obviously something strange was happening in the sky around Newcastle on the night of October 7."

This is an example of a mystery helicopter sighting which also conforms to more classic "UFO" sightings. The vast majority of mystery chopper sightings, however, appear to be normal terrestrial craft.

On the 5th of October in Alamosa County, Colorado, a black chopper equipped with a searchlight was chased by two police officers in their car. The same day a similar mystery chopper was seen southeast of Alamosa. From October 5th to October 9th in Alamosa County, unidentified helicopters were observed flying at numerous locations between 10:30 p.m. and 3:00 a.m. each night. Several of these choppers were noted to have very powerful searchlights.

In October 1975, A rancher in Sweetwater County in southwestern Wyoming (who was also a deputy of Sweetwater and Uinta Counties) was driving in southeast Uinta County when a dark green helicopter lacking identifying markings suddenly swooped into sight and began to pace his truck. The rancher tried to outrun the helicopter in a breakneck 90 m.p.h. chase. The rancher stated that the occupants of the helicopter were two long-haired men in cowboy hats who were laughing uproariously at his predicament. He also noted that there was a covering on the side of the craft which apparently concealed the chopper's identifying markings. The helicopter sped ahead of the truck and then landed in the middle of the road. The rancher stopped his truck, and then stepped out of the vehicle. Luckily he was carrying a shotgun in the truck. He fired three shots at the chopper as it sped away. The rancher's sighting was verified by a state trooper who also saw the helicopter.

On each night from the 13th to the 17th of October, again in Alamosa County, Colorado, an "Army green" mystery chopper flew west over the Great Sand Dunes National monument during the day, and returned via the same route at night. The chopper was said to sound like an airplane, rather than a helicopter.

Between October 30th and November 30th in Union and Quay Counties in New Mexico, there were a minimum of 30 chopper sightings. While the FAA announced that they were going to investigate these occurrences, they later denied any records of an investigation.

— During the Summer of 1975 in Douglas County, Colorado, an unmarked chopper landed for a short time approximately 300 feet from a house located near Franktown. The chopper was Army green and, curiously, was said to be constructed of solid metal, lacking a glass observation bubble (although this may have been a misidentification of a tinted bubble, which are often noted in black helicopter sightings).

— In Fall of 1975, in Washington County, Colorado, ranchers were reporting numerous mystery choppers and their connections to cattle mutilations. A rancher's daughter, at home by herself, observed a chopper flying over a field approximately 100 yards from her home. She described the sound of the chopper as "muffled." A dead cow was later found on the ranch. The rancher was stated to have believed that the animal had been lifted and then dropped into a pool of water from above.

— By November 1975 the Colorado "flap" had died off, although sightings of mystery choppers in Colorado (sometimes linked with cattle mutilations) would continue to the present day. Sightings during November are documented in Colorado, Wyoming, Montana, Texas, as well as a flurry of sightings in Maine, Massachusetts, and New Hampshire.

On the 2nd and 3rd of November in the Cascade, Chouteau, Pondera, and Teton Counties of Montana there were numerous sightings of unmarked choppers. At least two of these craft were seen over missile installations.

Again in Montana, on the 7th and 8th of November, this time in Fergus and Wheatland Counties, unidentified craft were seen over missile installations. The Strategic Air Command offered the information that, "the craft were suspected to have been helicopters due to hovering ability of the craft, witness interpretations of the sound produced and placement of lights on the craft."

In the first week of November, in Johnson County, Wyoming, residents spotted an unmarked helicopter with pontoon-style landing gear. Four calves were mutilated in the area about this time.

— In early December in Franklin County, Kansas, three large helicopters, "troop-carrier size," were observed landing near Lane. No further information is available on this sighting.

On the 8th of December, in the Cascade and Teton Counties of Wyoming, a number of "small dark-colored helicopters operating between 50 and 150 feet off the ground" were seen by residents and were chased by police officers in their cars. One sighting of these choppers was by a group of workers at a missile installation west of Chouteau. Announcements followed that the helicopters were possibly Canadian in origin, and were heading toward the U.S./Canadian border.

On the 16th of December in Lamar County, Texas, investigators on their way to the site of a cattle mutilation saw two camouflaged choppers in flight.

Mid-December in Cascade County, Montana, a crew at a missile launching site saw three mystery choppers flying above the installation at an altitude of 150 feet. A radio message was received at the sheriff's office stating that the choppers were from the National Guard, but an official of the guard later denied the report.

During December in Franklin County, Kansas, local deputies and the highway patrol pursued three unidentified helicopters which had first been observed on the ground.

Also during December of 1975, sightings of mystery choppers in Colorado continued to be numerous, although they abruptly dropped off at the beginning of 1976. One helicopter was observed to flash a light with an answer being flashed from a nearby mountain.

December of 1975 was the beginning of what mystery chopper researcher Tom Adams has called the Siege of '75' in northeastern New Mexico. Again, these unidentified choppers may have moved their base of operations after coming under too much scrutiny from public and the press.

In Colfax, Harding, Quay, and Union Counties a minimum of 30 mystery helicopter sightings took place in December, as well as four cattle mutilations. *The Tucumcari, New Mexico News* reported:

"James Gordon, Federal Aviation Adm. local Area Coordinator, announced late Wednesday (11-5-75) the FAA has officially entered into the investigation of the sightings of the air craft over northeastern New Mexico. At the present time the FAA investigators were in the field taking depositions from individuals who have actually seen these air crafts [i.e. black helicopters]." The FAA was later to deny that the investigation took place.

— During the latter part of 1975 over flights by unknown aerial craft took place over "sensitive military installations" in Maine, Michigan, North Dakota, and Montana. Craft were also seen over several missile silos in Montana, and in the vicinity of the Canadian Forces Station and radar installation in Ontario, Canada.

1976

— In Franklin County, Kansas, there were numerous sightings of unidentified helicopters throughout January, 1976. Dorothy Detweiler, living in rural Lane, observed three choppers, two which inexplicably hovered over her home for two minutes. Seven other families also reported the mystery choppers the evening of the 16th.

On the 26th of January, also in Franklin County, Kansas, Virginia Burkdoll observed a chopper with a blue-green light visible through its windows. "It didn't sound like any kind of aircraft she had heard before."

— During February and April of 1976 there were several sightings of unidentified choppers in Montana and Colorado.

— On the 31st of May in Elbert County, Colorado, a mutilated cow was found. Sheriff George Yarnell, responding to the report, saw an unmarked helicopter flying around the area, which then departed. Observers at the scene said that the chopper was flying at so low an altitude that they could see a number on it: N9143F, which was said to be registered to "City Car Terminal Company" of Detroit, Michigan, although I do not have information on any additional follow-up investigation.

— On unknown dates during May or June in Judith Basin County, Montana, up to twelve helicopters in pairs were observed in flight one evening. There were a number of other sightings in this area during this time period, and four cattle mutilations.

— Unmarked choppers were observed in Colorado, Montana, Kansas, and New Mexico in June, July, August, and September.

— In early Autumn of 1976 a hunter in the Red Mountain area near Norris, Montana saw a black helicopter without identifying markings fly overhead and then swoop below a low hill. The hunter climbed the hill and observed a black helicopter which he later identified as a Bell Jet Ranger parked on the ground. Seven men who apparently came from the chopper and were wearing civilian clothes were climbing the hill in the direction of the hunter. The hunter waved at the group and shouted greetings. Then, as he saw the group more clearly he was surprised to realize that the men were all Orientals, and speaking in a language he couldn't understand. The Oriental men turned and headed back to the chopper, and when the hunter attempted to follow, they started to run. They reached the helicopter with the hunter still in hot pursuit, and took off.

— During late September and early October in Las Animas County, Colorado, there were sightings of soundless choppers on four ranches. In one incident, four ranchers were herding cattle near Model, Colorado. Four helicopters — painted yellow and black, with tinted cockpit glass — flew in diamond formation toward the ranchers. Three of the choppers hovered in place, while another of the craft swooped down and scattered the herd of cattle. One of the ranchers displayed a rifle, and the single chopper rejoined the other three, and the craft then departed as mysteriously as they had appeared. The ranchers tentatively identified the choppers as Bell Jet Rangers.

On the 10th of October, 1976, in Wadena County, Minnesota, a silver and blue helicopter landed in a farmyard, and a group of children ran toward it, at which time the chopper immediately took off. On October 1st a mutilated calf had been found on the same property.

— During November and December of 1976, there were several sightings of lights and unmarked helicopters in Illinois and Colorado. There were also incidents of cattle mutilations in Illnois.

1977

— Reports of unmarked helicopters are scanty during 1977, although there are records of the choppers in Colorado, Arizona, and Texas (all of them linked to cattle mutilations).

1978

— In early January 1978 two choppers were sighted over a ranch in Perkins County, Nebraska. A mutilated bull was found in the same area the following day.

— In early June in Las Animas County, Colorado, there were two sightings of a single black helicopter. Two mutilation incidents occurred in adjoining Huerfano County in June.

— In mid-October on a ranch in Sublette County, Wyoming, a number of observers saw a white helicopter with a blue bubble flying by. A mutilated cow was later discovered on the ranch.

— On November 9th, 1978 in Benton County, Arkansas, Lt. Don Rystrom, a rancher who had served in the Marine Corps, was involved in the investigation of a number of cattle mutilations in the area. Rystrom heard a helicopter flying in from the east toward his ranch. The unidentified chopper flew across a pasture and then followed power lines, finally turning north to fly away. Rystrom only caught a glimpse of the craft but identified it as a dark-painted "Huey" with a single white light on the fuselage. The following night the helicopter was back. Following the same path that it had on the previous night, this time Rystrom was outside in time to train the spotlight of his police car on the craft, which accelerated northward and out of sight. Rystrom commented on the unusual "popping" sound that the helicopter made, rather than the usual sound of a helicopter.

On the 13th of November on the Santa Clara Indian Reservation two cows were found mutilated. A resident of the area stated that he had heard a helicopter on the morning of the 13th.

1979

— In January, 1979, in Eddy County, New Mexico five horses were mutilated. For a few days after the mutilations, choppers were seen in the area.

On April 8th, 1979, in Rio Arriba County near Dulce, New Mexico, police witnessed a craft which they thought might have been a helicopter hovering and playing a searchlight over a ranch where there had been a cattle mutilation. The craft rose without sound and flew over the mountains near Dulce.

— During May and June of 1979 four or five mutilations took place in El Paso County, in Colorado. At about this time, "dark" choppers were seen flying around area ranches and homes.

— On July 10th, 1979, in Fulkner County, Arkansas, Charles Reynolds found a mutilated calf on his farm, which he estimated had died two days prior, on the 8th. He had observed a helicopter hovering over his pasture on the 8th.

On the 21st of July, in Conway County, Arkansas, a cow disappeared at about the time that a mystery helicopter flew over the area. The mutilated cow was found on the 23rd, and witnesses noted that tree limbs above where the cow lay were broken.

— Again in Conway County, Arkansas, on August 12th, a blue unmarked helicopter was seen in an area where a mutilated cow was found two days later. Throughout August there were a number of cattle mutilations in Faulkner and Conway Counties, Arkansas, as well as sporadic sightings of unidentified choppers.

During the first week of August, 1979, a valuable bull was mutilated in Alberta, Canada. About a week earlier, a helicopter had hovered over the location where the bull was found.

1980

— In 1980 we see a dramatic reduction in the number of sightings of black choppers. On the 27th of October, however, in Apache County, Arizona, a mutilated and burned bull, appearing as if it had been "partially cooked in an oven," was found. Two or three days earlier an unexplainable beam of light had swept over the area. Later, on the 29th, a helicopter flew over the area where the bull had been found.

1981

— In Alberta, Canada, on the 28th of September, a mutilated bull was found. In the grass near the bull were three worn, triangular patches. A helicopter had been heard the previous night, and another was seen that day, as the mutilated bull was being examined.

1982

— On May 28th, a mutilated cow was found in San Juan County, New Mexico. An unidentified helicopter was seen hovering in the area on May 31st, and a small green chopper was observed hovering over the site of the mutilation on June 1.

— In El Paso County, Colorado, on September 29th, a chopper was seen flying near the site of a cow mutilation which had taken place on September 16th. Another mutilated cow was found later in the day on September 29th.

During late September and early November in Sweetwater County, Wyoming, and adjoining Daggett County, Utah, there were a number of cattle mutilations and associated mystery chopper sightings.

1983

— In Washington County, Colorado, on May 21st, 1983, a mutilated cow was found by a family of ranchers (reportedly the third "mute" that this family had experienced). A mystery helicopter hovering over the mutilation site was reported by a neighbor within two days.

1984

— On June 3rd, in an area reported to have had animal mutilations for over a decade, campers observed a black, unmarked chopper in King County, Washington. The chopper was identified as a "Huey."

1985

— On April 21, in Marshall County, Alabama, a cow mutilation occurred on a farm adjoining another where a mutilation had happened a year earlier. On a third adjoining farm a helicopter was heard the night after the mutilation.

— In El Paso County, Colorado, in late November or early December, a mutilated cow was found on Eldon Butler's ranch. The previous night Butler had heard a hovering helicopter near his ranch.

1993

— There seems to have been at least a partial hiatus in unmarked helicopter sightings during the period 1985-1993, but that was not to last. In 1993, there was a marked resumption of mystery chopper sightings, but the character of the reports had suddenly changed. Less often were the choppers seen in situations involving cattle mutilations, and more often were they seen in urban settings and flying in formation, or in the context of covert military maneuvers.

— In St. Louis Missouri, on March 5, five small black choppers were observed flying from the southeast to the northwest. Later the same morning three large "transport" choppers were observed traveling over the same house, going north to south. The middle craft of the group was described as a gunship. On March 17th, five black choppers pouring out black smoke were also seen over St. Louis, all described as "large gunships." The choppers were "unmarked, flat black, one behind the other, 300 to 500 yards off the ground."

— A letter reporting a black helicopter in Michigan was printed in the *Patriot Report* for March, 1993. As per the policy of the newsletter, the writer remained anonymous:

"Well, I found out today that the black helicopters are for real. If I had any doubts that there was such thing, that doubt was put to rest today. At 10:45 a.m. on 3/9/93, one went over our house at breakneck speed. We have commercial helicopters fly over almost daily. Believe me, there is no comparison. This helicopter, flying at about 500 ft. had pulled out all the stops. It was solid black, no definitive insignia or numbers on its fuselage, with the exception of three small white vertical stripes at the tail rudder; totally devoid of any other identifying marks. Obviously, at the rate of speed that it was going, it was not waiting around for anyone to come to that conclusion. Interesting enough, I could tell this was a helicopter of a different type than any commercial helicopter, as it was so noisy and its blade beating the air so loud that anyone must realize that this was not an ordinary helicopter. Its over flight lasted but a few seconds over our village. It came from the north-easterly direction, down M-60, possibly its origin from Ft. Custer, heading in a direction of the South Bend, Indiana direction. Again, I say it was solid black. Possibly of the Scorpion class, only larger. I would say this is not fun and games, Americans, something is going down, else why no markings and excessive speed?" Name Witheld, Michigan

— The following article from the *Stockton California Register* (3/4/93) entitled "Marines Practice Storming Stockton" attempted to put any fears to rest about impending "urban environment training" involving choppers:

"If Marine helicopters start buzzing your house today or tonight, don't be alarmed. It's only a drill. The 13th Marine Expeditionary Unit from Oceanside will conduct 'urban environment training.'

"For those who don't speak military language, that means about 2,000 Marines practice approaching an unfamiliar city with common street maps. In Stockton, the Marines will pinpoint buildings to get more familiar with the city.

"'People will not notice the training on the ground because we travel to and from sites in civilian clothes' said Marine Chief Warrant Officer Hartman Slate, a spokesman for the trainers. 'What they will see is the helicopters,' Slate said. The aircraft will include Cobra attack helicopters and the cargo and troop transport Super Stallion, 'the free world's largest helicopter.'

"At night, as they fly at the lowest point, about 20 stories high, you may hear the flying machines but not see them because they will be flying with their lights off and using night-vision goggles,' said Marine Sgt. Dave Hiersekorn."

—During July of 1993, there were multiple sightings of unmarked helicopters over Santa Rosa, California. Here is a news story from the *Santa Rosa Press Democrat*, dated August 9, 1993, by-lined Clark Mason:

"In a Whirl Over Mysterious Copters — DEA Agents Were On a Mission — Maybe.

"It took a week of phone calls to more than half a dozen government agencies, but finally the mystery of the low-flying military helicopters over west Sonoma County last month has been cleared up. Well, most likely cleared up.

"Contrary to popular opinion, the choppers that jangled nerves and spooked pets and livestock in Occidental, Camp Meeker, and Cazadero were not sent by the state's Campaign Against Marijuana Planting.

"'We're not active yet,' Said Dale Ferranto, a CAMP special agent in Sacramento. 'If anybody's flying, it's not a CAMP machine.'

"And although the flights were reported about the same time of former President George Bush's visit to the ultra-exclusive Bohemian Grove encampment, it wasn't Secret Service agents on those flights.

"A California National Guard spokesman said even if the helicopters belonged to the Guard, there was no way of immediately determining their intent, because they fly in support of 75 different law enforcement agencies.

"'You need to get the right office doing the mission,' said National Guard Major Ron Hooks. 'If they want to, they'll tell you what they're doing.'

"Sonoma County Sheriff Mark Ihde said his department was not involved. The sheriff said the first he heard about military helicopters disturbing west county residents was when he read it in the newspaper a week ago.

"Ihde said the federal Drug Enforcement Agency held a training school in Sonoma County two-and-a-half weeks ago and used eight or nine fixed-wing aircraft provided by the Civil Air Patrol. But to his knowledge, no helicopters were used.

"Maurice Brown, a DEA spokesman in San Francisco, said the agency used National Guard helicopters in Sonoma County as part of an LSD bust earlier in the Summer, but he was unaware of any recent operations in Sonoma County.

"But as it turned out, some of the denials appear to be a case of the left hand not knowing what the right hand was doing because the choppers were indeed supplied by the National Guard in conjunction with a DEA exercise.

"Sonoma County Undersheriff Dale Moore said the Guard helicopters were used to ferry agents in and out of marijuana gardens in the Geyserville area and other northwest areas of Sonoma County. Even though Moore doubted the helicopters were in the Occidental area, irate citizens had no doubt they were. The residents questioned why they were flying over a relatively populated rural area where they were unlikely to find pot gardens of any consequence.

"Ed Barr, an Occidental business consultant, said he was sitting outside with a client, a former Vietnam veteran, who got some instant bad memories when the airships showed up.

"'They were like two helicopter gunships. They appeared over the rise. It was like slamming him into the Vietnam experience,' he said. 'They kept circling overhead.'

"Cathy Weeks, a woman who lives between Cazadero and Duncans Mills, said a big, drab olive Huey chopper with a red cross painted on its front flew over her home July 20 and kept circling, only 200 feet above her house. 'It kept flying around and around for 45 minutes,' she said. 'It was uncalled for. I didn't know if there was a lost child or a fugitive. It was real low... my two dogs got so freaked out they ran off and didn't come back for a few hours.'

"Weeks said the helicopter was so close she could see the clothes of its occupants, including one mustachioed man with sunglasses dressed in civilian clothes. He was dressed in stonewashed jeans and a light blue golf shirt.

"'I could pick the guy out of a line-up,' she said, adding she tried to call and complain later, but could get no one from the National Guard to acknowledge the helicopter.

"Capt. Stan Zezotarsky, spokesman for the Army aviation branch of the Guard, confirmed that his agency's helicopters were used in Sonoma County July 19-23 in conjunction with the DEA office in Sacramento.

"'Periodically we have observation school, training school, how to compensate for the effects of flight in spotting marijuana from the air,' he said. 'We provided three helicopters to do that.'

"Zezotarsky said while a court order stipulating flights must be above 500 feet recently expired, his agency still tries to stay above that altitude.

"Walt Smith, chief of the Sonoma County Airport Tower, said National Guard helicopters were at the airport for four days two-and-a-half weeks ago. There was a big Huey, and two OH-58 observation helicopters belonging to the California National Guard. There was also a National Guard fuel truck. The crew, based at Mather Air Force Base, talked about the DEA being with them.

"But Smith could not explain why west county residents were still complaining about low over flights last week, after the National Guard choppers had already left the area.

"Undoubtedly confusing matters is the presence of a smaller private blue-and-yellow helicopter that continues to be used in an ongoing logging operation in the Harrison Grade area.

"Or the choppers last week could be from yet another branch of the military with similarly colored flying machines on another anti-drug mission.

"A spokeswoman for the Sixth Army at the Presidio in San Francisco said Friday that she was able to verify the 14th Aviation Group of the Army Reserve did fly an anti-drug mission in Sonoma County last week. She referred a reporter to a public affairs officer in Southern California for further details. That officer was not available for comment."

— During September of 1993, in Priest Lake, Idaho, a black helicopter hovered 50 feet above a cabin, observed by a resident of the cabin, then the chopper moved off and hovered above other cabins in the area. It is said that there were many military aircraft flying low over Priest River during the same period of time, and were often seen headed north toward Priest Lake.

— During the Summer of 1993, residents of Midtown Atlanta, Georgia were shocked in the early hours of the morning as three military helicopters came churning through their high-rise condo canyons.

Marsha Brown, living at the 27-story Colony Towers, said that the sudden appearance of the choppers was "frightening and sort of terrifying." Brown watched the dark, unmarked choppers fly across Atlanta's central plaza, and then rise to hover over the Colony Square building. "In the canyon of Peachtree Street, the extremely loud sound... echoing off the buildings, well, it is a terrible-sounding thing," Ms. Brown said.

"I can't imagine any circumstance that would authorize that kind of activity in an urban, or a residential area. I don't think anything warrants this kind of situation, short of war."

There were numerous complaints about the black chopper flights and Atlanta Police Major Wayne Mock responded: "Special Operations Command units conduct urban-training exercises about four times a year, but not always involving helicopters or aircraft."

The Special Operations Command was back in Atlanta in July of 1994, although this time they left the helicopters behind, perhaps for public relations reasons. *The Atlanta Journal,* dated July 12, 1994 described what took place:

"ATLANTA: Midtown Explosions Part of Military Training.

"The 'automatic weapons fire' and explosions that echoed around an abandoned state office building on Peachtree Street in Midtown Saturday afternoon, cracking a window in a nearby business, was a military urban training exercise, according to Atlanta Police Maj. Wayne Mock, head of special operations, said military units he would not identify performed 'simulated hostage rescue and life saving' exercise for several days late last week. He refused to provide details except that the training, in contrast to similar, larger scale maneuvers in Midtown last summer, did not involve helicopters. Employees of a Kinko's copy center at 793 Peachtree St. Saturday saw men in battle gear atop the 800 Peachtree Building and heard the sound of gunfire from the building when a window cracked from 'a bullet or a bomb fragment,' said Kinko's employee Tom Roberson. Mock said neither Atlanta police nor state law enforcement agencies were involved in the exercise, only military. The Defense Department will pay for the damage to the window, acting through the APD, Mock added."

If these were regular maneuvers, why was Major Mock unwilling to provide details to the press, or to identify the military units which were involved?

The APRA News describes another tactical maneuver involving black helicopters in Georgia:

"In August of this year [1993], the U.S. Marine Corps shocked and disturbed suburban neighborhoods in Stone Mountain, Georgia as they flew military helicopters low over private residences in the middle of the night. The UH-1 and CH-46 choppers, which are based at Camp Lejeunne and New River Station, North Carolina were conducting urban drills in Dekalb County. In one such operation they made a noon-day flight from Dobbins Air Force Base to a simulated hostage situation at a motel near the intersection of Interstate 20 and Candler Road."

— In late 1993 in Lewis County, Washington, near Mossey Rock, a man stumbled across a black helicopter which had landed on a remote section of his property. Men from the chopper were walking nearby, and he was ordered by them to leave that area of his land and to keep his mouth shut about the sighting. No further information is available on this incident.

— Beginning in April 30, 1993, the mysterious chopper sightings took a new turn. The following story is reprinted from the *Patriot Report,* June 1993:

"According to reports from American citizens around the nation, military aircraft have been seen spraying over certain residential areas and particular remote targets where patriots live. The reason helicopters and fixed wing aircraft have been spraying those scenes is unknown...

"— A man in St. Maries, Idaho reported seeing a military jet on April 30, 1993 over a residential area. It had two unusually shaped canisters near the wing tips. It came over slowly at approximately 1000 ft, sprayed something, then banked and quickly left the area. Birds were found dead in the area following the spraying.

"— A twin engined aircraft flew low over Noxon, Montana spraying something last fall, a few weeks later a 2 year old boy died from a mysterious illness.

"— Peyton, Colorado land owners fighting with the Federal Housing Authority to keep their land have been sprayed numerous times by black helicopters. They report becoming deathly ill in addition to losing 10 cattle, 7 dogs, and finding 28 deer dead on their property. The local sheriff traced the helicopters back to the National Guard in Denver, Colorado. (the National Guard denies spraying the ranchers' property.)

"— A doctor noticed some spraying by aircraft south of Couer d'Alene, Idaho. He took an air sample and a sample on a plant. He tested these samples in his lab and found them to be 'biological.' He said that he had never seen anything like it, and it may have been genetically altered (We are waiting for documents on the lab test results.)"

An incident of a similar nature took place on May 19, 1994, near Trout Creek, in Montana: Two unmarked jet aircraft crisscrossed a valley in this area. A woman who had watched these jets became ill with what were described as "radiation" symptoms. Within one day, all of the woman's pets and chickens (approximately 175 of them) had died.

1994

The following story is reprinted from the *Patriot Report*, dated February 1994:

"Dallas Home Erupts in Flames after Helicopters Flew Over.

"Michael Benn, the initiator of the petition to impeach President Clinton, was rudely disturbed by the sound of military helicopters at 6:40 a.m. Tuesday, January 11th. Black helicopters with their side doors open, flew suspiciously low over the neighborhood twice. On the second pass the neighbor's home across the street was engulfed in flames. Other neighbors reported hearing a loud roar and seeing rockets or missiles being fired at the roof of the house. At 7:30 a.m. a white flatbed truck arrived and for some unknown reason took out all the appliances and electrical items. At 9:30 a.m. a white van drove up and a man dressed in white coveralls started going through the rubble. Four holes were reportedly seen on the roof with white powder residue around them. The fire marshal said that the cause of the fire was not lightning, and there is an investigation on-going at this time.

"This incident was reported on short wave radio on January 21st when Tom Valentine interviewed Michael Benn during the Radio Free America broadcast. He believes that the helicopter attack was supposed to have been on his home but the attackers targeted the wrong house. He has just collected his 12,000,000th signature for the petition to impeach Clinton, and believes it is quite possible that someone wanted him out of the way."

In the *Thatcher Thunders!* newsletter, R.G. Thatcher talks about his own mysterious chopper sighting which took place in east Texas:

"On Wednesday, January 19, 1994, upon hearing the loud clak-clak of an approaching helicopter, I stepped out of my little study building to see a Soviet Mi-8 Hip helicopter fly over the north front of my family's property, which is located about seven miles south of Richards, Texas. It was initially flying from east to west. It was 12:55 p.m. The sun was out. I was shocked to see one, not that I wasn't mentally prepared for such an eventuality. You see, I've talked and written about Soviet Communist aircraft — big transports, jet fighters, and military helicopters — flying our skies under various pretexts since 1990. I make it a habit to visually inspect with binoculars every noisy helicopter and big aircraft that flies low over my area during the day time. I, however, did not have my binoculars handy, but that didn't matter. The helicopter couldn't have been more than 175 to 200 yards away. The alarming problem with this helicopter was that it was flying less than 100 feet off the ground. It was flying NOE (Nap of the Earth) — this is considered the safest technique to minimize observation by enemy ground observer or radar but it is also the slowest method. This technique requires it to fly at very low level and fly around objects rather than over them, weaving just above, when unavoidable, and between the tree tops — not going along a straight course higher above them. The helicopter was painted in two-tone camouflage colors of pale green and tan. I feel the helicopter was trying to minimize its exposure to both people on the ground and radar. By the time it got over my next door neighbor's large front yard, it turned in an approximate northwest direction."

— During the beginning months of 1994 black helicopters and jet transports, all lacking markings, were reported and confirmed by other witnesses to be flying in the Okanogan, Ferry, and Stevens County region of northeast Washington.

— In May, 1994, in Carson City, Nevada, a flat black or olive drab OH-58 Kiowa (Jet Ranger) chopper hovered over an urban area for 20 minutes. There were no markings on the craft, although an "infrared pod or minigun" was observed on the fuselage.

On May 7th, in Harrahan, Louisiana, a teenager who was home from school was chased for 45 minutes by a black helicopter with a rope hanging down from it. The persons in the chopper pointed "scopes" at the teenager, which he thought were weapons. A report was made to the police chief in Harrahan, but he indicated that the chopper was owned by the federal government, and that he lacked any authority to do anything about it.

During the second week of May, persons travelling in a car on Highway 395 near Spokane, Washington, were chased by a black chopper. The craft travelled with the car for several miles, hovering above it, and when they tried to elude the chopper by turning off the road, a rope ladder was dropped and men in black uniforms carrying weapons began to descend. The driver immediately drove the car back onto the highway, and increased traffic is believed to be the reason that the chopper then departed. Also seen in May was a Russian Hind chopper on the ground at the McDonnell-Douglas facility in Phoenix, Arizona.

— In late June or early July heavy black helicopter movement was reported near Knoxville, Tennessee. A witness reported "constantly" seeing black gunships flying toward Oak Ridge, Tennessee, and that they flew from two to eight at a time, "low and fast."

— On July 19, 1994, at Center Senior High School in Kansas City, Missouri, a charcoal black twin-rotor Chinook spiraled downward over the school to an altitude of 100 feet, and then circled the athletic field for 13 minutes.

— During the first half of 1994 residents of the San Luis Valley of southern central Colorado saw "swarms" of black helicopters appearing over their homes and places of business. These craft lacked any identifying marks which might have given a clue to their source. These craft are reported to have been flying about the area and buzzing homes for about two years. These flights seem to be originating from and returning to the estimated 100,000 acre Baca Ranch, although no reconnaissance has as of yet been done to find out where the choppers are stationed within the ranch.

— During October and November, black helicopters which lacked any identifying markings were observed in Dartmouth, Massachusetts, overflying the University of Massachusetts. To counter the alarm of the students and local residents, messages were flashed on local televisions and computer screens assuring them that military helicopter training was taking place. Reports were received of helicopters flying so low that local residents could make eye contact with the pilots.

— Black helicopter flights have also been regularly seen for the past several years over Napa County, California, flying out of Hamilton Air Force Base. The choppers are reported by reliable sources to have been supplying a sophisticated secret base on Bureau of Land Management property near Oakville Grade. Aerial reconnaissance of the area shows that the base includes concrete bunkers, a newly-built road, what seem to be openings into an underground facility, and eight to ten microwave dishes apparently used for satellite communications.

Asked to comment on the black helicopter traffic by Harry V. Martin, editor of the *Napa Sentinal* newspaper, an Air Force spokesman simply said that, "The helicopter traffic over the Napa Hills is a classified operation."

In an article in the *Napa Sentinel,* "Mysterious Black Helicopters Stalking Nation," Martin reported:

"In the Watsonville area, one such helicopter landed. Law enforcement officials went to investigate but left the scene when encountering armed men in black uniforms. 'We had black helicopters come over here everyday,' state several Massachusetts families. 'They were just plain with no markings.'

"These type of helicopters have also been reported over Loring, Maine, Wurtsmith, Michigan, and Malmstrom, Montana, as well as northeastern New Mexico. Military officials in Colorado state that black helicopters seen in their areas do not belong to the military...

"The bulk of the helicopter traffic is seen throughout the United States from August through October, with some heavy activity in February, July, November and December."

— At least fifteen black helicopters (identified by witnesses as Bell OH-58D(i) Kiowa Warriors) are currently, as of Summer 1994, performing night missions out of the National Guard Base in Tupelo, Mississippi. The helicopters were flown to the military base by members of C Company, 1st battalion, 185th aviation, from the Bell helicopter facility in Fort Worth, Texas.

These choppers are equipped with the most high tech of electronic surveillance equipment, including infrared digital laser trackers for tracking targets in the dark, and rocket pods capable of firing Stinger missiles for eliminating those who are tracked. According to one source who has been watching the Tupelo base, the helicopters generally carry two crewmen in black battle uniforms which lack insignia.

— During the latter part of 1994, observers on either side of the Canadian border have watched dozens of black helicopters said to be flying out of the U.S. Army's Fort Drum in upstate New York, to destinations beyond the Canadian border. It is known that there are large numbers of Army Black Hawk helicopters located at Fort Drum, and these conform to the descriptions of the black helicopters which have been observed. Fort Drum is also the location of a great deal of activity in the way of "urban warfare" training, which will be discussed later. One ominous note for those concerned about recent threats to American national sovereignty is that Canadian troops have repeatedly been seen at the Fort Drum military base, training with members of the U.S. 10th Mountain (Light) Division.

— One area where there has been a tremendous amount of black helicopter activity in 1994 is Michigan. Mark Koernke (a.k.a. "Mark from Michigan), formerly an intelligence analyst and counter-intelligence coordinator for the Army, in the video *America in Peril,* informs us that, "Many people have witnessed their activities all over the state... Many of our allies and friends in the northern part of the state have seen virtual waves of helicopters. Not five or six, but any four nights in a row we have seen from 34 to 50 helicopters in waves, going from horizon to horizon not in column. In one particular evening, with four people standing back to back, there were so many aircraft that the four could not count them all...

"Considerable activity has taken place in the thumb of Michigan and some of our people checked this out with people who live in the area. They said, 'Oh, yes, we've had a lot of crashes here.' Has anybody seen anything in the media about crashes in the thumb? They refuse even to talk about it. We have queried state authorities. They do not respond, yet they advise us there have been at least five specific air crashes. Five! A helicopter is not a small thing to land in your backyard, especially in your pool or something.

"What are the helicopters used for? Control and command, tracking and tracing... for actually tracking your car. Tracking and tracing is very difficult unless you have something to track and trace with."

The same source, Mark Koernke, relates, "...this is an ongoing program that you are not seeing in the general media. The campaign, however, is intensifying. During the earlier phases, for instance in Chicago, the black helicopter missions... were taking place extensively. We had individuals in high-rises who were above the helicopters flying between the high-rises in Chicago, in the windy city. These operations culminated in a final activity that lasted about one week in which they cordoned off neighborhoods, went from building to building, and house to house, entering the houses forcibly if necessary to prosecute the owners if any ammunition, firearms, or gun parts were found. This was 'Operation Clean Sweep,' an activity that was covered only by National Public Radio."

One source for the black helicopters may have been revealed by Koernke. He has stated that in 1990 approximately 3,000 rotary winged aircraft were withdrawn from the strategic reserves of the U.S. These helicopters were owned by the Air Force, but were purchased from them using tax dollars, then transferred into other unspecified hands. This source states that the helicopters withdrawn from American reserves were both heavy lift aircraft and attack helicopters. The ones that Koernke has observed flying in Michigan he has identified as Chinook CH 47's (which were painted black). This is a double rotor craft which can carry 64 soldiers at a time.

— During the latter portion of 1994, a group of over 80 black helicopters passed overhead near New Orleans, Louisiana, startling the locals as the choppers headed toward some unknown destination. The flight of choppers was later described to a military analyst, who guessed that this might have been an aerial transportation of as much as a brigade of troops.

— In another incident, a black chopper with a white U.N. insignia was spotted near Thompson Falls, Montana.

— In late 1994, *The Lewis River News*, in Woodland, Montana, published the following story by Norm Olsen, titled "Are There Secret Doings on Woodland's Dike Road?"

"Last week, Wednesday to be exact, a young man called *The Lewis River News* with an odd story he didn't want to keep to himself. These mysteries are always difficult for a newspaper to deal with because the source may be a crackpot or a practical joker or just someone who may have misinterpreted what he or she saw or experienced.

"Almost always such tales are heard politely and the source told we will look into it and we come up empty-handed. That would have happened this time, but for the fact one of our staff members also remembers Army helicopter gunships in this area last week.

"So let's get on with what happened. He was on vacation from Kansas and visiting locally, he said, and at about 11 a.m. he was traveling on the Dike Road when he saw two helicopters in the distance. They were black. He said he is familiar with the Army's Black Hawk and these appeared to be bigger. One was distant and the other was closer, close enough for him to see an open side door and two crew members inside.

"There appeared to be a weapon in the door and it seemed there was another on a mount that pointed forward. The helicopter was moving around in circles. So he turned off the road and crossed a bridge. He stopped just on the other side of the bridge and got out of his car with his camera and took several photos. As he was getting ready to leave he was accosted by two U.S. Army sergeants who wanted to know what he had been taking pictures of. He told them. They asked him how many photos he had taken, and he said three or four. They demanded that he turn over his camera and film to them.

"The young man, in his mid-20s and a former serviceman himself, began walking to his car when one of the pair said he couldn't leave until he turned over the film, which he did. The sergeant opened the camera, removed the canister and pulled out the film. He then put the exposed film and canister in his pocket and returned the camera.

"'It kind of made me mad,' he said, 'I had pictures on that roll of my vacation; you know, the Rockies, Yellowstone Park and things like that.'

"As if this incident isn't just a little weird already, the young man described the car the two were driving as a white Dodge Intrepid with civilian license plates. Other than having a cellular telephone antenna, it was a plain vanilla car.

"Asked if he could take us to where all this happened, he said, 'Sure, be glad to.' He did and of course there was no white car, buck sergeant, sergeant major or helicopters to be seen. All he could do was point out where the Intrepid had been parked, where he had parked, where he had seen the aircraft, and where the sergeants had stopped him.

"So what does all of this mean? Was the young man delirious from the scorching 73-degree Washington sun? Did the choppers spot him and call the sergeants? Were the sergeants just out for a drive, in uniform on the Dike Road, and then decide the guy with the camera, nearly out of sight to anyone who doesn't know the road, shouldn't be taking pictures of Army helicopters? Who knows?"

Connections of black helicopters with cattle mutilations seem to have confused the issue — perhaps purposely — about what has been taking place in thousands of mysterious chopper incidents for over 20 years. What is apparent is that at least a substantial number of the sightings are of aircraft involved in covert government operations on domestic soil. This has become more apparent over the past few years. In my book *Casebook on Alternative 3*, I talk about little-known aspects of cattle mutilations:

"There are additional clues that are not often mentioned in the popular media. Many 'mutes' have been found to have been marked with fluorescent paint, probably as an aid to identification in the dark. A large percentage of mutilated cattle have also been found to have been injected with strains of harmful Clostridium bacteria (of which blackleg and malignant adema are members of the genus). In an investigation of bacteriological warfare in 1970, Senator Frank Church's Senate Select Committee on Intelligence determined that the CIA had stockpiled canisters of this same bacteria.

"One persistent rumor has been that cattle are used in biological testing due to the similarity of the membrane of the eye with that of a certain ethnic group. Researcher Ed Sanders interviewed G.C Errianne, a former member of an unspecified intelligence agency, who admitted that secret bacterial research was being conducted in the United States and that these researches were targeted 'in regard to Oriental warfare.' Sanders also interviewed reporter Bill Hendrix of KTVX-TV in Salt Lake City, who confided that Dugway Proving Ground in Utah had done research on a specifically anti-Oriental biological weapon."

The answer to a substantial percentage of the cattle mutilations is most likely what the evidence points to: secret testing of biological warfare viruses. This would also offer a clue to the precision cuts which are sometimes observed in the mutilations; if anyone is likely to be in possession of the kind of laser or other high technology tools necessary to create these kinds of incisions, then it would be the government.

Faulty observation by witnesses may also explain a significant percentage of anomalous sightings, while government testing of advanced secret craft would explain an additional percentage of incidents. I am not willing to absolutely rule out the possibility that some of these sightings of black helicopters might have something to do with UFOs of the truly alien variety, as many researchers have suggested — in my research I am not willing to rule out the possibility of virtually anything — but it is quite possible that the government is also spreading stories of flying saucers in order to confuse what is actually taking place. We know for a fact that they have done this in certain instances, as I document elsewhere in *Casebook on Alternative 3*.

Certainly we know that almost all of the black helicopters which are being seen around the country currently are government craft, dispatched from one agency or another. Recent reports suggest, in fact, that within the last year or two virtually all military aircraft have had their service insignia removed (with the singular exception of the Coast Guard). What is the reason for that? It has been suggested these craft are being prepared for incorporation into the United Nations military command, although this is not the only possible explanation.

According to a story in *The Spotlight* newspaper, "Today almost all of them [military aircraft] are painted what has become known as 'neutral United Nations dull gray' and bear no markings other than the small tail designator letter and a small bureau number that appears beneath the horizontal stabilizer at the tail of the plane.

"Some helicopters are reportedly painted flat black, dark gray or dark green but do have insignia rendered in a glossy finish of the same color, which, according to one source, is a special paint that can be detected by infra-red detection devices, apparently for identification by friendly forces.

"Readers can quickly detect the absence of insignia by spending some time around any U.S. Air Force facility, watching the arrival and departure of various aircraft. While at low levels over the airfields it can be readily seen that the aircraft are painted the dull gray and bear no insignia.

"To illustrate the extent of U.N. influence over the U.S. military services most aircraft of foreign countries still bear their national markings. It would appear that the United States has marched farther down the road to the U.N.'s New World Order than much of the rest of the world."

WELCOME TO THE NEW WORLD ORDER!

DETENTION FACILITIES AUTHORIZED THROUGH FEMA AND AUGMENTED BY DOD BUDGET AMENDMENT PASSED WITH 1991 FISCAL BUDGET

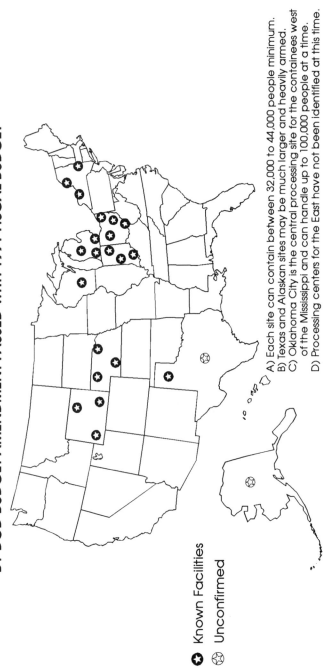

A) Each site can contain between 32,000 to 44,000 people minimum.
B) Texas and Alaskan sites may be much larger and heavily armed.
C) Oklahoma City is the central processing site for the containees west of the Mississippi and can handle up to 100,000 people at a time.
D) Processing centers for the East have not been identified at this time.

⭐ Known Facilities
✪ Unconfirmed

HH-GOA Night Hawk Black Chopper
Currently being extensively deployed in the U.S.

AH-64 Apache

AH-64 Apache Black Helicopter
Employed extensively in covert missions in the U.S.

MJTF (Multi-Jurisdictional Task Force) Police Locations

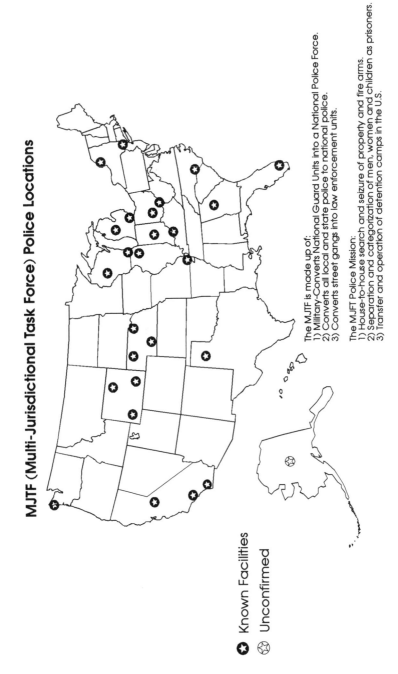

The MJTF is made up of:
1) Military–Converts National Guard Units into a National Police Force.
2) Converts all local and state police to national police.
3) Converts street gangs into law enforcement units.

The MJFT Police Mission:
1) House-to-house search and seizure of property and fire arms.
2) Separation and categorization of men, women and children as prisoners.
3) Transfer and operation of detention camps in the U.S.

✪ Known Facilities

⊛ Unconfirmed

Black Cobra Gunship

Likely Locations of Concentration Camps

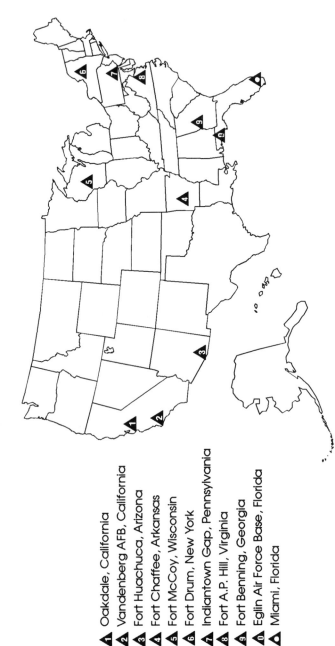

▲ **1** Oakdale, California
▲ **2** Vandenberg AFB, California
▲ **3** Fort Huachuca, Arizona
▲ **4** Fort Chaffee, Arkansas
▲ **5** Fort McCoy, Wisconsin
▲ **6** Fort Drum, New York
▲ **7** Indiantown Gap, Pennsylvania
▲ **8** Fort A.P. Hill, Virginia
▲ **9** Fort Benning, Georgia
▲ **0** Eglin Air Force Base, Florida
▲ Miami, Florida

2

Men and Machines

As the black helicopters are whirring over our cities and countryside (I personally have seen several fly over my own house, located in a suburban area of a major western city), there are other even more ominous things happening that are connected to these events. Although — yet again — you will not hear anything about these events on television or in the Establishment-controlled press, there have been troop movements and training activities, along with large shipments of war materiel, many involving vehicles of foreign manufacture, taking place within the border of the United States. These secret military operations are extremely difficult to explain in terms of U.S. security, especially considering the supposed dismantling of the Soviet war machine.

1992

In May of 1992 a training course was conducted at the First International Crime Conference in Fairbanks, Alaska. The name of the course was Police 2000. The trainees at this course were police officials from America, Canada, and Russia, and one of the purposes of the course was to assist in the creation of a "transnational police organization for the coming global village."

— In August of 1992, a C-130 military transport plane lacking identifying markings landed on the Yaak River Road in rural northwest Montana. An observer saw 60 soldiers in black uniforms leave the plane, along with 15 pack mules. The soldiers fell into two lines, and their commander gave them orders in a foreign language. One of the words that the commander used was "*nyet.*" Within 15 minutes the plane had taken off, and the men marched up a road that led to an old World War II fighter base that had been out of operation for many years, and had been off limits to the public.

The "abandoned" base does, however, have a decrepit airfield. There has been speculation that the mission of the soldiers may have been to refurbish this airfield. Over the next six weeks the C-130 returned two more times, while on the third landing on September 5, the soldiers and the mules were taken back into the plane and departed. Recent roadwork in the area was confusing to the local residents, since it was done in a rural area that was used very little by the public. Now the reason for the roadwork seems more clear.

Near the site of the troop landings there is a National Guard Base, located on Turner Mountain. Double rotor Chinooks had been seen flying in this area for several months. There is speculation that these choppers are flying from Malmstrom Air Force Base in Great Falls, Montana, and from the base at Turner Mountain.

1993

— The following is a transcript of the 6 p.m. News Report, on KTSM TV, El Paso, Texas, for February 18, 1993. Reporter Mark Pettinger:

"The German Defense Minister Ruag who is still inside the German Air Force Air Defense School is here to check up on his troops to see what kind of training they are getting now that there are 500 soldiers stationed here at Fort Bliss in the Air Force. This was German Defense Minister Ruag's first visit to the facility here at Ft. Bliss. He was in Washington, D.C. yesterday to talk to U.S. Secretary of Defense Les Aspin about the new role for the United Germany in defending the world. The German constitution prohibits Germany from taking part in certain activities in terms of staging their soldiers. The defense minister would like to see German forces take part in U.N. missions and already in other parts of the world they are taking part in peacekeeping missions."

German Defense Minister Bolker Ruag: "I think we owe it to our self-respect that we take the same risks as others do in the Alliance. We've begun to do that. I'd like to point out that we do have medical soldiers in Cambodia at the moment, and that daily we fly into Sarajevo with planes. One was almost shot down last week."

Reporter Mark Pettinger: "That's why the German Defense Minister says that the training of his troops get here at Ft. Bliss is very important. This is just one of 54 locations across the U.S. where German troops do train. Now the German Defense Minister is headed to South America, specifically to Chile and to Argentina where they are going to check up on military efforts down there and see if they can incorporate some of the training for their forces back in Germany."

—Beginning in February of 1993, there were repeated sightings of foreign troops in Montana, and the likelihood is that they weren't there just to sightsee. 1,500 troops were spotted in the Lincoln, Montana area, during the time in which they were involved in exercises with the Montana National Guard. Six soldiers from Nepal signed a guest book at a store in Lincoln. Another observer saw "several hundred" foreign troops doing parachute jumps near Lewistown, Montana.

It is reported that many roads leading into the wilderness in Montana have been widened, and there are reports of military convoys on Highway 93, headed toward Idaho.

The Helena Independent Record reported that Forest Service lands in Montana would be used in exercises by foreign troops during the coming summer.

The Patriot Report, in covering the story, stated that, "The arrival of foreign troops wouldn't have bothered American patriots if it wasn't for the fact that this scenario was uncovered years ago as a strategy to control and police American citizens. If an economic collapse occurs in the future along with civil violence and martial law, U.N. troops would be utilized as an additional force to confiscate firearms and police America. If this happens, it is an act of war against America and all patriot Americans should prepare to defend their nation."

The Montana operation cited above may have been part of "Operation Shadow," which took place in Montana beginning on May 17th. Confirmation of these training operations with foreign troops came in the form of an article titled "Operation Shadow," by Kimberlee Lincicome, in the October 1993 issue of *Continental Marine*, published by the Department of Defense:

"The Army cordially invited a Marine Reserve reconnaissance unit to Helena, Montana, for a joint service training exercise known as 'Operation Shadow' May 17 - June 5.

"Bravo Company, 4th Reconnaissance Battalion graciously accepted the rare opportunity to gain some multi-national training.

"'Our unit needed more experience with long-range patrols, mission planning and night tactical inserts,' said Captain John Stone, inspector-instructor with B. Company, 4th Reconnaissance Battalion in Billings, Montana...

"Operation Shadow's overall mission was to provide coalition warfare training to the joint services and cross-train with international forces according to Forward Operational Base Director Lieutenant Colonel Craig R. Firth, executive officer for the Army's 10th Special Forces Group, 3rd Battalion...

"During the exercise, the Recon Marines was tasked with conducting realistic, advanced patrols of (8 or more days) without resupply in various points throughout the mountains.

"In addition, they utilized long-range land navigation and communicated with the Surveillance and Reconnaissance Center (SARC) with HF near vertical incidence skywave (NVIS).

"NVIS is an advanced system of communication in which transmissions bounce up to 75 miles over mountains according to Stone.

"One of the training highlights was night tactical insertion by Army Black Hawks [helicopters] from TF (Task Force) 160s. Using night vision goggles, pilots and crew members were able to insert and extract Marines in complete darkness.

"Because a participating Belgium paracommando's unit has a projected deployment to Somalia in August, they were eager to gain some hands-on experience from the recon unit.

"'We've been looking forward to jumping with the American Marines,' said Belgium Lieutenant A. Lteruen, commanding officer with 3rd Bn, Paracommando in Tielen, Belgium...

"The Canadian Forces also seemed to respect and admire their leatherneck counterparts...

"Indeed, because 'Operation Shadow's' mission was performed well and beyond many of its participant's hopes, the exercise may be expanded next year on a larger scale depending on specific factors."

— On May 1st and 2nd of 1993, Air National Guard C-130 transport planes from a number of states landed at the Orlando, Florida International Airport. A Boeing 747 aircraft from Belgium also landed and Belgian troops disembarked to subsequently be picked up by the Air National Guard. Black C-130 aircraft were also flying in the Orlando area during the same period of time.

— Edwin Young, the editor of *Contact* magazine, was given information by friends who traveled by car on Route I-17 in

Arizona on September 10, 1993. While driving along the highway they passed about 40 to 50 Arizona National Guard, U.S. Army, and white United Nations vehicles (ranging from troop carriers to "humbees") traveling in convoy, and led by a United Nations command car. They also noted a military-enforced checkpoint at Cordes Junction. Later that night 20 more vehicles in convoy were seen along I-17. Also noted was the fact that black Apache attack choppers were "all over the area."

— In the *Omega Times*, it was noted that convoys of foreign soldiers were seen moving through the Arkansas area during October of 1993. Most of the troops and equipment were camouflaged and lacked identifying markings, although some of the troops wore the blue helmets of the United Nations. The *Omega Times* reported that 15 combat groups of UN soldiers had been confirmed in the area.

1994

— In March of 1994 near Rye Gate, Montana, and the Lewis and Clark National Forest, a train was seen transporting 100 flatbed cars carrying Russian military vehicles. These included BMP-40 armored cars equipped with 75 millimeter cannons (used for urban warfare), Russian UAZ-469B jeeps, and what were apparently ZIL-131 and KamAZ 5320 heavy trucks. Also on the flatcars were American M113 armored personnel vehicles, painted white and bearing the insignia "U.N."

In March 1994 the Coast Guard fuel depot at Port Smith, Virginia was placed under more stringent security. A local resident sneaked into the depot and saw Russian armored military vehicles "as far as the eye could see." He also saw helicopters being loaded onto barges.

—On May 9, 1994, an 18-wheel flatbed truck carrying Russian jeep-style vehicles painted white was seen in Riggans, Idaho. Five cartons labeled as containing poisonous materials were also strapped to the truck.

This fax, dated May 29th, 1994, was printed in *Contact* magazine:

"Urgent:

"Yesterday... at approximately 6 p.m. — Over 100 flatbed railroad cars passed through Johnstown, PA and visual count took place at an area called 'Horseshoe Curve.'

"The flatbeds contained tanks and armored vehicles of many kinds. This train was heading West out of Johnstown, Pennsylvania, which is one of the three main railroad spurs in the eastern part of the United States.

"One old-timer (individual) who witnessed and saw the railroad convoy stated; 'The last time I saw anything like this, the United States went to war.' He also remarked that it was the largest train of war vehicles he had ever seen... even larger than what passed through Johnstown in World War II, Korea, or Vietnam.

"All equipment was 'O.D. [Olive Drab] Green' and the train convoy came into Johnstown, Pennsylvania from the northeast direction. Johnstown, Pennsylvania has three main spurs — one goes south, two go west. All military movement on rail must go through Johnstown.

"*This is a confirmed sighting and count number.* James Wickstrom."

— In June 1994 a report was received that a highway in Mississippi was blocked while a convoy of military trucks either entered or left Camp Shelby, a National Guard facility. More importantly, it is reported that the buildup of armored vehicles at Camp Shelby is greater than it has been than at any time since World War II.

Also in June 1994, three barges were seen carrying heavy armored tanks and other military vehicles up the Mississippi River. The oil rig worker who witnessed the shipment stated that the vehicles were of unknown but foreign origin.

A dock worker informs us that in June of 1994 he unloaded white painted Russian trucks at the Port of Gulfport in Mississippi. These trucks were equipped with a wide variety of items, including hookups for water cannons and equipment used for cleansing the air during nuclear or biological warfare. The dock worker's nephew noticed a strange box with a light on it attached to one of the trucks, and the facility was immediately shut down with the CIA summoned to the site. One of the CIA men was overheard saying, "We didn't think they had anything that sophisticated." There has been some guesswork that the box may have been a satellite uplink, although this has not been confirmed. The dock worker indicated that the intended destination for the Russian equipment was California.

In June of 1994 a report was received from a retired military man about a storage area near the Pearl River in Columbia, Missouri, containing 200 Soviet Russian T-72 tanks.

In June 1994 a brigade of elite, rapid-deployment soldiers from the U.S. Army's 10th Mountain Division, stationed at Fort Drum in northern New York were transported to Fort Polk, Louisiana where they took part in two weeks of "advanced readiness" training. Fort Polk is currently operating under joint command of the U.S. Army and the United Nations. As noted earlier, Fort Drum is the probable base for numerous black helicopter flights which have been observed in Canada.

The training reportedly involved familiarization with techniques of "urban warfare" such as house-to-house searches, just the sort of skills which would be required if these troops were used to subdue the American populace rather than, for instance, bandits in Somalia or homegrown dictators in Haiti. Actually, I'm not certain if I see a tremendous difference between a Haitian dictator and recent American presidential administrations. It would seem to only be a matter of the effectiveness of their public relations.

Members of the same 10th Mountain 's 10th Signal Battalion also took part in a 12-day training exercise at Fort Indiantown Gap, Pennsylvania, from June 11 to 23, 1994, involving 10,000 military personnel. This exercise was mounted in conjunction with FEMA (the Federal Emergency Management Agency), an agency whose assigned sphere of operations is the United States. A further indication that the Fort Drum troops are not being trained for assignments in foreign countries is that the Fort Indiantown Gap base where they are training houses an elaborate center for exercises in urban warfare, a model American town named "Johnson City." Fort Indiantown Gap is also one of a number of locations which were designated by FEMA planners as detention centers during a national emergency center.

The Spotlight newspaper for June 6, 1994 offered a pointed question about the Fort Drum base:

"Why was a base covering a wide expanse of northern New York, near the St. Lawrence River, which separates the United States from Canada, chosen for a rapid deployment unit, designed to be sent to various trouble spots that could be expected to occur in the deserts of the Middle East and the tropical climate of Central America? ...The location of the base has given rise to speculation among Canadians that the light division was stationed just across the border in northern New York for some secret Pentagon plans for operations in Canada."

Another possibly relevant piece of information is that in March of 1994, the Canadian government indicated that it would close its military training college at St. John, located near Montreal — and that the facility would be turned over to the United Nations. There have also been reports that other Canadian military bases have been turned over to the United Nations.

The following is a *Militia of Montana Intel Report* for June 22, 1994. The incident is dated June 15, 1994:

"Junction with I-59 [apparently Meridian, Mississippi or Birmingham, Alabama], men in black uniforms with ATF [Bureau of Alcohol, Tobacco, and Firearms] on the back, in black vans; a lot of them did not speak English and those who did spoke in broken English; shut down east and northbound lanes of the interstate, searching for 'illegal weapons'; these weapons were supposedly on a truck coming from Texas, having passed through Louisiana."

— As noted in *The Patriot Report* of July 1994:

"Topic: Russian/East Bloc T-72 Tanks in West Texas. Date: June 12, 1994. Location: IH-10 Westbound lanes, marker no. 258. Proceeded to exit and crossover and parked the semi trucks in the furthest east section of the Exxon truck terminal cafe parking area. This is directly adjacent to U.S. Highway 285 at the northwest edge of Ft. Stockton, TX. Two semi trucks, two very large trailers, and a T-72 [Russian] tank on each of these. Both truck tractors were solid white color [as per the UN color scheme], and on each door had a decal, rectangular in shape, 'Trism Specialty Carriers,' no address. Tanks: Definitely T-72 with full gear, the only item visibly absent was the 12.7mm heavy machine gun, of course, stowed. Spare fuel drums were at the rear of the rear deck, and all else appeared combat ready. One T-72 appeared new or to have been completely refurbished and had a dark green/greenish gray camo scheme. The other T-72 had a more weathered look, light green/tan/dark green camo. A two digit number was seen on this one, whereas the number 'A30' was stenciled in white, relatively small, above the track and on the left front corner of the dark T-72. No unit or national markings were observed. Departure time unknown, destination unknown. It is speculated that they would resume travel west on IH-10 to El Paso and beyond. There are no military installations between Ft. Stockton and El Paso, distance 240 plus miles."

In June of 1994, the National Guard were also expanding their sphere of influence — and their ability to engage in illegal, unconstitutional search and seizure. In the June 30th, 1994 issue of the *Washington Post* an article details some of the Guard's recent activities in Puerto Rico:

"Residents of 50 high-crime housing projects have awakened to the blasting of chopper blades and the crush of combat boots this past year, as pre-dawn raiding parties of police and National Guardsmen have turned their neighborhoods into occupied territory...

"The Guard's deployment [in Puerto Rico] marks the first time the soldiers have been used for conventional crime fighting. The house-by-house takeovers have won the praise of Clinton Administration 'Drug Czar' Lee P. Brown (who toured some occupied Puerto Rican housing developments in May), although Brown conceded that Americans 'in other localities may not be as amenable.'"

On the other hand, when has the government worried about whether the people are amenable?

— In Spring 1994, near Biloxi, Mississippi, hundreds of white-painted, Russian-built military vehicles (including vehicles used for chemical and biological warfare purposes) were being kept in a depot surrounded by barbed wire and guarded by attack dogs. *The Spotlight* newspaper, investigating the importation of foreign vehicles into the U.S., were able to obtain bills of lading for Russian vehicles obtained from East Germany, shipped through Gulfport, Mississippi docks, and then transported to the depot. The vehicles listed on the bills of lading included several kinds of Russian ZIL heavy trucks, including biological and chemical warfare decontamination trucks. The bills of lading also indicated that the vehicles were bought for the U.N.

A large road, about 35 feet wide, has been built from the truck depot, connecting it with the Stennis NASA Space Center, approximately 20 miles southeast of the truck depot, near the border of Mississippi and Louisiana. Other reports say that the Russian vehicles are being shipped by barge in this area, via the Pearl River, although there is no indication as to where the shipments are headed.

Also received was videotape of an area of the public airport at Gulfport, Mississippi used by the National Guard. The video showed Russian helicopters including Mil-24 Hind-D and Ka-27 Helix types, parked amid dozens of American helicopters. Unconfirmed reports suggest that flights are taking place nightly by U.S. helicopters to two Russian naval ships located in the Gulf of Mexico in an area designated as "off limits" by the U.S. military.

Also during the Spring of 1994, a Soviet Frog surface-to-surface missile was seen being transported by truck and trailer on Interstate Route 1 in Louisiana. The Frog can carry virtually any warhead (including nuclear) and has a range of 37 miles.

— On July 10, 1994, in Dallas, Texas, six "Deuce 1/4 U.S. military vehicles" along with a number of camouflage-painted trucks with red crosses were seen, with the last vehicle in the convoy bearing a blue U.N. flag. The trucks were carrying equipment and supplies. One truck also carried between 15 and 20 soldiers.

— As of July 1994, 600 U.N. troops wearing black uniforms and blue armbands were reported to be stationed in the area of Dulce, New Mexico. This is an area with a long history of black helicopter sightings and cattle mutilations, and has also been implicated in numerous tales of government collaboration with extraterrestrial entities, suggesting that the government disinformation masters are working overtime to conceal the actual activities taking place in this vicinity. A single government disinformation agent putting out tales of space aliens and alien-government collaboration can confuse and render unbelievable other reports of actual government activities, such as advanced flight testing, biological labs, and underground bases. I would caution all readers to carefully assess reports linking extraterrestrials with government secret activities, and to ask who might benefit from report like these.

On July 12, 1994, a Russian SA-8 anti-aircraft missile system (a "Gecko," by NATO designation) was spotted as it was being transported on U.S. Route 64, near Winchester, Kentucky. Twelve missiles of the SA-8b series were also being transported, six of them carried in the launching tubes on top of the vehicle. These missiles can reach an altitude of eight miles, and carry a 40 kilogram warhead.

— The August 3, 1994 issue of the *Augusta Chronicle*, in Augusta, Georgia, described the landing of a 300 Marine contingent in black helicopters on Tybee Island, North Carolina. Mallory Pearce, a local resident said that the appearance of the Marines was "A real invasion. I was scared and mad." The Cobra gunships carrying the Marines descended toward Pearce's house and then hovered above it.

"The housetop was rattling, a tree branch fell in my yard and troops came rushing through my property with guns drawn," Peace said. "They were hiding in bushes with weapons. I presumed they were loaded. I went outside and told the people in charge to stop this, that it was tearing up my property. One of them handed me a claims sheet and said to fill it out if I had any damage, but that they couldn't stop the exercises."

According to a spokesman for the Marines, Lt. Jeff Jergensen, the black helicopter invasion was meant to "provide Marines the opportunity to practice" in a situation resembling ones where U.S. citizens might need to be rescued.

When Pearce informed the Marines that what they were doing on his property was "unconstitutional," Pearce was told to "get out of a restricted area."

— On August 21, 1994 a Soviet Tupolev TU-20 heavy bomber and a Soviet jet used for mid-air refueling identified as an Ilyushing IL-76 landed at Barksdale Air Force Base in Louisiana. Thirty Russian Air Force officers also arrived with the planes. Barksdale AFB is located approximately 100 miles from Fort Polk, which is alleged to be the North American Training Center for U.N. Command forces. Shortly before the arrival of the Soviet planes, a Russian Hind helicopter was observed three miles from the Barksdale Base, flying toward it.

During August of 1994 reports were received of "hundreds of thousands" of Soviet small arms, ranging from pistols to machine-guns, which had been confiscated from Iraqi soldiers, being brought to the United States. Given the anti-gun stance of the Clinton administration, why are these guns being stockpiled in the States?

Also in August of 1994 plans were announced by the U.S. Army for a simulated invasion of Ranier, Washington by Special Forces paratroopers from nearby Fort Lewis. The "invasion" of Ranier was slated for September 22. A dozen paratroopers would parachute into Ranier, armed with rifles equipped with laser sensors and firing blanks, and the paratroopers would be met by 170 members of the National Guard in a simulated urban combat situation.

When residents of Ranier heard about the planned "invasion," a town hall meeting of 1,300 persons was held, and the consensus was clear; the citizens wanted the exercise called off. Faced with the public opposition, the Army canceled the maneuver.

In August of 1994 a report from Dwight Kinman was circulated on the *American Patriotic Fax Network*. Kinman stated that, "The New World Order crowd and Clinton are moving rapidly toward the One World Government. This is a documented fact: Our powerful radio station (KXL) in Portland, announced on August 2, 1994, 7:05 a.m., that 'Russian troops are being brought into Oregon to fight our raging forest fires.' Our Governor Barbara Roberts would not permit our National Guard to fight the fires, but would call for Russians to be brought in.'"

Here is a report from the Posse Comitatus group of Ulysses, Pennsylvania, dated August 16, 1994:

"TENNESSEE: 6 August 94.

"At approximately 1 p.m. on above date, approximately 21 black helicopters were sighted at the local airport in Smyrna, Tennessee [located approximately 20 miles from Nashville].

"Five of the 21 helicopters were Soviet and displayed a large red star on each craft. These five Soviet helicopters were described as 'weird' and 'funny shaped' and the tail sections had what appeared as 'legs' protruding.

"The Smyrna, Tennessee airport has a National Guard [unit] there. These black helicopters were guarded by two men in a blue automobile... One of the guards spotted our intell source and said source went to the local radio station to inform them to go to the airport with a camera for a news story. These 21 black helicopters departed immediately.

— In September of 1994, Soviet T-72 heavy battle tanks were seen near Pendleton, Oregon. No information has been obtained on what the tanks were doing there.

Also in September, a huge "anti-drug" raid was carried out by state troopers in the Kenai Peninsula, near Anchorage, Alaska. The state troopers ignored the nicety of search warrants, but still insisted on entering the homes of residents, in some instances with truckloads of Drug Eradication and Interdiction Unit members of the Alaska National Guard waiting outside. When Armin Schmidt of Kasilof, Alaska, told the troopers that they couldn't enter his home without a search warrant, he was told in true Orwellian style that he would "be investigated." Alaskan State Police Sergeant Wayne Bortz justified the unconstitutional actions by saying, "if it's all bogus [anonymous reports of drug possession], nothing's here, then we're out of your hair. If you're not committing a crime, there's probably no problem if I come in." I wonder if Bortz would have felt the same way if his own home had been one of those to be invaded by troopers?

Bortz indicated that 12 persons had refused to let the troopers enter their home, and that "Investigation into activity of those homes is continuing."

— In Summer of 1994 word was received that the Clinton administration had come up with the bright idea of mixing the training of American and Russian troops at bases in the United States. The reasoning behind this joint training was not indicated. Although there was no word as to the number of Russian troops which would ultimately be involved in this co-training, this information may be a signal that major operations are about to take place, since this kind of joint training has apparently been going on for years without virtue of a press announcement. Recent reports have placed Russian troops in Alaska for joint training in chemical and biological war, as well as in other locations in the United States.

This announcement of joint training may be related to a delegation of seven members of the United States Senate who recently traveled to Russia, headed by Senator Sam Nunn, the chairman of the Senate Armed Services Committee. The U.S. delegation engaged in talks with Russian officials over joint American and Russian training, ostensibly meant to assist in U.N. peacekeeping efforts. The Russians made it clear to Nunn and the rest of the U.S. delegation that 250 U.S. troops were not welcome in Russia, but the American group were quite accommodating in agreeing to the training of Russian troops on American soil.

— As of late 1994 reports were arriving fast and furious of curious troop movements and materiel shipments in the United States. The following are a just few of these reports:

A Marine Sergeant reports that there are 40,000 U.N. troops based in San Diego. A report issued from Anchorage, Alaska states there are 14,000 U.N. troops stationed there. "They are black uniformed, have black vehicles and semi-automatic rifles." Harry Martin, of the *Napa Sentinel* newspaper, reports that there are 50,000 U.S. National Guard or U.N. troops stationed near Barstow, California.

Reports have recently been received of United Nations troop movements in Arkansas, as well as U.N. troops involved in maneuvers in the Ozark National Forest. An anonymous observer quoted in *Leading Edge* magazine reported that there were training maneuvers taking place near Sacramento, California which involved joint deployment of the U.S. Marines and the FBI. This, the observer reported, was part of a scheme to transport street gangs such as the Bloods, Crips, and Guardian Angels to different urban areas and to use them as storm troopers to raid private houses and to conduct searches for the confiscation of guns. This may not be quite as far-fetched as it sounds. Recent reports in the above-ground press have talked about millions of dollars of funding being provided for ghetto gangs by the government — in one instance, 2.5 million dollars for a single gang in Detroit — with large portions of the monies being quickly confiscated for their personal use by gang leaders, or used to buy weapons to further consolidate their gang's territorial control.

In late 1994 a group of three trains, all carrying white-painted military vehicles, were seen stopped at a crossing near Wheatland, Wyoming, 60 miles north of Cheyenne. An Air Force officer viewed the trains while they were stopped at a crossing, but due to poor night time visibility, he was not able to identify the cargoes, beyond saying that they were armored military vehicles. The officer did say, however, that the trains were guarded by soldiers dressed in black uniforms.

A small convoy of Russian military vehicles were seen traveling east near the Utica exit in upstate New York. Five train-loads of military vehicles have arrived at Fort Chaffee, Arkansas, bringing the number of armored vehicles stockpiled at Fort Chaffee to between 2,000 and 3,000 vehicles. Informants have noted a recent shipment of 5,000 mattresses to the Fort Chaffee facility, and that there is a large quantity of barbed wire stockpiled there. A great deal of unspecified construction activity has also been taking place at the military base.

Callers to short wave radio talk shows in the latter half of 1994 have reported troop maneuvers in Idaho which included camouflaged armored personnel carriers and trucks bearing Federal Emergency Management Agency insignia. It was said that the personnel carriers and troops were directed by uniformed men carrying large signs with arrows, making me think that these exercises may have included soldiers who could not speak English (or read U.S. maps), and also that the troops were not relying on radio communications.

Other reports over the short wave have said that Belgian U.N. troops have been seen in North Dakota and Montana, German troops are reported as being seen in Texas, and there are reports of Russian troops in Alaskan operations and chemical warfare training with American troops in Alabama.

The Spotlight newspaper noted that an urban warfare training center has been built near Fort McClellan in Alabama, and that it is designed to duplicate the appearance of a small American town, right down to storefronts with American names like "Ribeye Restaurant." This has caused some to wonder whether the training is intended to prepare troops for urban warfare conditions in America. Armored vehicles located at the base have been painted white, the traditional color for U.N. vehicles. One photo taken of the base shows a German TPz-1 light armored car, used in ferreting out biowarfare and chemical agents during warfare. It is reported that there are up to a dozen of these German military vehicles located at this base. Also reported is that Russian troops (or possibly troops from another East European country) have been engaging in training maneuvers at this facility.

Naturally, the government denies that these troop movements, training activities, and shipments of military equipment are taking place in the land of the semi-free and the home of the apathetic. Senator Conrad Burns, of the Department of the Army, when confronted with information about the shipment of Russian tanks and other vehicles in his home state of Montana directly denied that such things existed. He said, instead, that these were Canadian vehicles which were used during the training of Canadian troops in the United States "under the umbrella of the United Nations." Senator Burns did not address widespread concerns by Americans that this umbrella would do nothing to hold back the rain.

In addition to numerous reports of troop and materiel movements (and the selection that I have included here is only the tip of the iceberg of reports), there are also reports of "detention centers" being set up in the country. Is this the piece of the puzzle which will cause all the others to fall in place?

3

Concentration Camps

The secret government plan dubbed Operation Rex 84 came into being at the confidential orders of President Ronald Reagan, and authorized the setting up of at least 23 huge American concentration camps (or "emergency detention centers") to be used in case of a national emergency. Under the Rex 84 contingency, plans were developed for the arrest of "suspect aliens" as well as troublesome homegrown elements considered "potentially subversive," numbering in the tens of thousands. Although the National Security Decision Directives that brought these camps into being have since been canceled, the concentration camps are said to still exist.

Twenty-three camps were originally commissioned via Rex 84, with an additional 20 camps funded through 1990-91 military allocations. In addition to the 43 detainment centers which were commissioned, there are other supplementary facilities which exist nationwide, or which are in the process of being commissioned.

If you are inclined to think that all of this information is made up, I will offer the official view on the subject of American concentration camps. This information is excerpted from the *CRS Report for Congress,* prepared for members of Congress by the Congressional Research Service of the Library of Congress. In the briefing paper titled "Current National Emergency Issues: A Brief Overview" (document 94-596 GOV), under the heading of "Relocation and Detention Centers," it is stated: "Finally, past Federal Government creation of relocation and detention centers during emergency situations continues to be of public interest. Several weeks after the United States formally entered World War II, President Roosevelt issued E.O. 9066 of February 19, 1942, which effectively ordered the internment of individuals of Japanese ancestry living in the U.S. By early August of that same year, some 110,000 Japanese-Americans — fully 70,000 of whom were legal citizens of the U.S. — had been detained and incarcerated in so-called relocation centers in accordance with the President's order. Congress subsequently sustained the internment order in an act of March 21, 1942, ratifying and confirming E.O. 9066 by making any action in violation of the restrictions laid down by the President, the Secretary of War, or designated military subordinates a misdemeanor punishable by a $50,000 fine and one year in jail. For the most part, the internees remained in the relocation camps until the surrender of Japan and the end of World War II. Many years later, the injustices perpetrated against the internees were officially investigated and verified, and legislation establishing a procedure and conditions for granting them redress was adopted.

"One of the earliest post-World War II delegations of emergency power occurred with the Emergency Detention Act, which was Title II of the Internal Security Act of 1950. According to section 102 of the detention statute, the President, in the event of an invasion of the U.S. territory or possessions, a declaration of war by Congress, or an insurrection within the United States in aid of a foreign enemy, could declare an 'Internal Security Emergency,' which would make effective special police power provisions of the statute. The Attorney General could 'apprehend and by order detain each person as to whom he, the Attorney General or such officer so designated, finds that there is a reasonable ground to believe that such person may engage in, or may conspire with others to engage in acts of espionage or sabotage.' The individuals, who were to be detained until the termination of the emergency or appropriate legal action had occurred. Detention centers were maintained at former Army installations in Avon Park, Florida, Tulelake California, and Wickenburg, Arizona. There was also a detention center at the Allenwood, Pennsylvania, ordinance depot.

"In 1968, when riots were devastating various urban centers of the Nation, two references to detention centers heightened public apprehension about them. The first arousal occurred in response to a congressional committee report which said that acts of overt violence by 'guerrillas' in the United States were analogous to a 'state of war' and might justify the use of the detention centers 'for the temporary imprisonment of warring guerrillas.'

"The use of the term 'guerrillas' was regarded by some to be a cryptic reference to black urban rioters. This suspicion was given popular support when a novel by John A. Williams gained wider readership. Actually published in 1967, *The Man Who Cried I Am* discussed, in the context of its own story, a secret governmental scheme called the King Alfred Plan, by which black Americans would be incarcerated in special camps. This fictional situation coincided in the minds of some with the detention suggestion made in the congressional committee report. Undoubtedly, this was not the only stimulus prompting calls for the repeal of the Emergency Detention Act, but it did serve to mobilize opinion in favor of such action. In 1971, Congress enacted legislation overturning the detention center statute."

What the authors of the CRS Report are not in a hurry to tell you is that, regardless of whether the Emergency Detention Act was overturned, the facilities themselves were not dismantled.

Although personal on-site investigation should be done to verify the following information, camps and "detainment facilities" are alleged to exist in at least the following locations: Camp A.P. Hill, Virginia; Fort Chaffee, Arkansas; Fort Drum, New York; and Fort Indian Gap, Pennsylvania; Oakdale, California; Eglin Air Force Base, Florida; Vandenberg Air Force Base, California; Fort McCoy, Wisconsin; Fort Benning, Georgia; Fort Huachuca, Arizona; Wickenburg, Arizona; Elmendorf Air Force Base, Alaska; Eilson Air Force Base, Alaska; Tulelake, California; El Reno, Oklahoma; Tulsa, Oklahoma; Florence, Arizona; Camp McCoy, Wisconsin; Maxwell Air Force Base, Alabama; Mill Point, West Virginia; Allenwood, Pennsylvania; and Camp Krome near Miami, Florida.

Sites of other alleged detention camps include two facilities located at the NASA facility in Mississippi. These camps, we understand, are currently being used for Haitian refugees and for prisoners from the Sheriff's Department in Hancock County. One report suggests that the Marines have been busied at the nearby Pearl River, clearing away logs and other debris for the stated purpose of bringing submarines up the river.

Researching the plans for concentration camps during the 1970s, Dr. William R. Pabst described additional sites:

"Here are the designated sites: tucked away in the Appalachian Mountains of central Pennsylvania is a bustling town of approximately 10,000 people. Fifteen to twenty years ago it was a sleepy village of 400. Allenwood, Pennsylvania is linked to New York City by Interstate U.S. 80. It takes up approximately 400 acres and is surrounded by a 10-foot barbed wire fence. It now holds approximately 300 minimum security prisoners to keep it in shape. It could hold 12,000 people from one day to the next.

"Thirty miles from Oklahoma City on U.S. 66 is El Reno, Oklahoma with an approximate population of 12,000. Due west, 6 miles from town, almost in sight of U.S. 66 is a complex of buildings which could pass for a small school. However, the facility is overshadowed by a guard house which appears to be something like an airport control tower — except that it's manned by a vigilant, uniformed guard. This is a federal prison camp or detention center. These camps are all located near super-highways or near railroad tracks or both.

"The federal prison camp at Florence, Arizona could hold 3,500 prisoners. It is presently kept in condition by approximately 400 legally convicted prisoners.

"Some of the other locations are: Tulelake in California — now in private hands. Some of the others: 'We have Mill Point, West Virginia. At Montgomery, Alabama we have a federal civilian prison camp at Maxwell Air force Base... There's one at Tucson, Arizona, David Munson Air Base...'

"And that brings us to a facility in Florida called Avon Park. I sent a representative to see what was at Avon Park, Florida. He found the Avon Park bombing and gunnery range, which is also listed as the 56th Combat Support Squadron of the U.S. Air Force; which is also listed as the Avon Park Correctional Institute. No one is permitted entrance and probably there is no overfly."

Pabst further reported that, "The cadre of specialized persons to enforce this [concentration camp] plan are found in the U.S. Army Reserves - Military Police Prisoner of War Command at Livonia, Michigan. Mr. Fennerin of the 300 Military Police POW Command at Livonia told me, when I called him from the Federal Information Center at Houston, that the camps in the command were for foreign prisoners-of-war and for 'enemies of the United States.' I asked him if enemies of the United States included U.S. citizens. He became angry, wouldn't deny it, and referred me to a very sinister individual at the Army Reserve facility here at Houston who I talked to who explained to me that the prisoners were called "inventory" and "internees." He would not deny that the camps were for U.S. citizens.

"I called the Pentagon, spoke with the defendant there, and then with the provost marshal for the Fifth Army, and do you know what? Not one of these persons would deny that the system was for U.S. citizens. The provost marshal for the Fifth Army — when I mentioned the names of all the camp sites — said, 'Well at least you've got that right.'

"The names of the detention facilities that I gave him were a list that I had acquired from the *Ozark Sunbeam* [newspaper]. That list of names was the same list of facilities designated under the old Detention Act of 1950 as 'emergency detention centers.' But there is only one problem: That act was supposed to have been repealed in 1971. After some research, I found out what the problem was. One congressman — when the hearings were held for the repeal of the Emergency Detention Act — mentioned that there are 17 other bits of law that provided for the same thing. So it didn't matter whether they ever repealed the Emergency Detention Act. The public was in fact tricked by the Congress of the United States!"

An additional list of detention camps has been formulated by researcher Jeff Thompson in his study of FEMA (Federal Emergency Management Agency) maps. He states that each of these sites can hold between 32,000 and 44,000 people, and that they share other similarities. Thompson informs us that: "They all have a large body of fresh water. They all have a train system within 5 miles or closer. They all have a major highway relatively close. They all have a major airport relatively close. But for all of these transportation systems all in one area, these locations are inordinately uninhabited (with the exception of a couple)."

"These locations are:

1. Cokeville to Kremmerer, Wyoming, in west of state/Absaroka Ridge with Fontanelle Creek and Reservoir/Interstate 80 and train/airports at Rock Springs, Wyoming and Salt Lake City, Utah on I-80.

2. Sheridan/Buffalo, Wyoming/Lake De Sniet/Interstate 25 with train to Sheridan; airport at Sheridan/Oil fields.
3. Wheatland, Wyoming, north of Cheyenne/Wheatland Reservoir and Sybille, Laramie and North Laramie Rivers/Interstate 25 and train; airports at Cheyenne and Laramie down I-25.
4. Yankton/Vermillion, Nebraska, north of Sioux City/Missouri River/Interstate 29 nearby, U.S. 20 and 81; train to Sioux City; airports at Yankton, Sioux City, and Norfolk, Nebraska.
5. Chadron, Nebraska in northwest Nebraska/Niobrara and White Rivers/U.S. 20 and U.S. 385; train to the southwest; airport at Chadron and Alliance, Nebraska.
6. McCook, Nebraska in southwest/Republican River and Swanson Lake/U.S. 83 and U.S. 34; train; airport in McCook, Nebraska.
7. Amarillo, Texas/Lake Meredith/Interstate 40, U.S. 87/I-27; lots of trains; large airport. This may be a very significant place because there are UN and MJTF [Multi-Jurisdictional Task Force] troops there already.
8. Rothschild, Wisconsin, Big Eau Pleine Reservoir/U.S. 51 and U.S. 10; train to nearby Stevens Point; airport at Mosinee north on U.S. 51.
9. Near Paoli, Indiana in south central portion of state/Patoka Lake, East Fork White River/Hoosier National Forest/Interstate 64 and 65, and U.S. 150; trains to north and to east down U.S. 150; airports in Evansville, Louisville, and Bloomington.
10. Terre Haute, Indiana, to the south of Terre Haute/Wabash River/I-70 and U.S. 41; trains to north, south, east, west; airport in Terre Haute.
11. Fort Wayne, Indiana - Huntington, Indiana/Maumee River/Huntington Lake/I-69 and U.S. 30; trains everywhere; airport in Fort Wayne.

12. Kalamazoo, Michigan - Niles, Michigan or Benton Harbor/St. Joseph River, Dowagiac River, Lake Michigan about 25 miles/I-94, I-80, U.S. 131, U.S. 12; a lot of train connections; airport in Benton Harbor and near Kalamazoo.

13. Midland, Michigan, south of Saginaw Bay, close to Freeland/Pine and Saginaw Rivers/I-75; train to the airport or nearby.

14. Dundee, Michigan, south of Detroit/Raisin and Huron Rivers/I-75 and U.S. 23; train; airport near Southgate.

15. Defrance, Ohio/Maumee River/U.S. 24; lots of trains; airport at Maumee, Ohio.

16. Ashtabula, Ohio, in northeast corner of state/Lake Erie and Grand River/I-90; lots of trains; airports in Euclid, Cortland, Warren, and Erie, Pennsylvania.

17. Coshocton, Ohio or Newcomerstown/Walhonding River/I-77 and I-70, U.S. 36; train, but no close airport.

18. Portsmouth, Ohio/Scioto River and Ohio River/U.S. 52 and U.S. 23; train, but no airport. Rickenbacker AFB is far to the north.

19. Batavia, New York/I-90, rivers and trains galore; airports at Depew and Greece.

20. Hudson, New York/Hudson river/I-87; trains; airport at Poughkeepsie.

21. Gouverneur, New York/Oswegatchie River/trains; airports in Watertown and Ogdensburg.

22. Brounwood, Texas/Lake Brounwood and Bayou River/U.S. 183 and U.S. 67; train (one goes through Fort Hood); airport.

23. Fairbanks, Alaska/Nenang River/Star Route 3 from Anchorage; trains; airport;/Fort Wainwright: Army."

Another source of information about concentration camps is Canadian journalist Serge Monast, the author of a book called *The United Nation's Concentration Camp Program in America* (which was unavailable to me at the time of this writing). I was able, however, to obtain a copy of a press release from the *International Free Press Network* which included an excerpt from an upcoming book from Monast. Although some of the details of Monast's account sound unlikely, I am including this information on the basis of providing the most complete reporting of the subject possible. The reader is cautioned about the need for confirmation of this information. Monast writes:

"We do know that the military-industrial complex and various federal government agencies have constructed and are working in many installations, underground bases and detention facilities; some of them accommodating large numbers of people at very deep underground [levels], and quite sophisticated. According to the latest reports such deeper facilities may be several hundred feet underground. Tunnels could be as large as 50 ft. by 50 ft. in diameter and chambers as much as 100 ft. high. In some installations truck or railway traffic might be important. Two-track railroad or two-lane highway tunnels [are] as much as 31 ft. wide by 22 ft. high. Camouflage has been considered. Under the direction of FEMA much work, including a great deal by the Corps of Engineers, has been done to design and construct underground or earth-covered key facilities, and also underwater special facilities along the Atlantic and Pacific coasts of the U.S., as well as in the Great Lakes region. We also learned from covert sources that there are similar deep underground facilities in Canada, Sweden, Switzerland, France, Saudi Arabia, Israel and Russia. FEMA and the Pentagon administer at least 50 secret underground command posts around the U.S. We have been informed that the NORAD base is also the 'National Warning Center' for FEMA. This is the place from which warnings for Canada and [the] U.S. are to... round up people under United Nations Authority. The command center is jointly staffed by both Canadian and U.S. military personnel. the NSA (National Security Agency) operates with computers which are engaged in a massive surveillance of much of the world telephone, telex, fax, radio, TV and microwave communications, including surveillance of domestic, internal U.S. communications by ordinary citizens. Ninety-six secret FEMA underground bases and facilities are located in Pennsylvania, Maryland, West Virginia and North Carolina. And we are not talking about LASL's unusual underground lab (Los Alamos National Laboratories [in New Mexico]) for instance. We also know that they extended underground bases and facilities as deep as 6,000 ft., but [it] looks like they even reached 8,000 ft. deep. We have maps, official documents, designs and exact locations of deep underground bases and detention facilities; pictures of equipment used for tunneling technology; information concerning underground structures; designs and construction; the flame-jet tunneling system; the high-temperature protective suit designs, and more...

"Some, and we say only some of the approximate locations of those underground bases and detention facilities are situated in: Kennesaw Mountain, just outside of Marietta, Georgia, and Green Mountains on the outskirts of Huntsville, Alabama. Other 600 ft. diameter cavities up to 4,000 ft. below the ground are located in Kingman, Arizona; Mohave County, Inyo County, California; Argus Mountains near Darwin (Argus Park); Mesa and Montrose Counties, Colorado (Sinbad and Paradise Valleys); 40 miles southeast of Moab, Utah; Pershing County, Nevada, in the Shawave and Nightingale Mountain ranges; Mesa County, Colorado in Unaweep Canyon 30 miles southwest of Grand Junction; Emery County, Utah, 10 miles south of Gree River; Winkler and northern Ward Counties, Texas, near... Kermit and Wink; Mohave County, Arizona, northwest of Kingman; Franklin County, Alabama, near Gravel Hill; Kansas and Nebraska, granitic basement areas; Oglethorpe and parts of Greene, Wilker and Elbert Counties, Georgia, near Highway 77 and the Georgia railroad; Chira Lake Naval Weapons Center, under Argus Park, California; Prince William Sound and the Kenai Peninsula, Alaska; southwestern Minnesota; Santa Barbara, California; Keweenaw Peninsula, Michigan; area of Cornwall, Pennsylvania; Vermillion Cliffs, Coconino County, Arizona; Grand Washington Cliffs; area of Barbeton, Ohio; area of Rifle, Colorado; Morgantown, West Virginia; area of McConnelsville, Ohio; Logan County, Illinois; Kunia, Hawaii; near the small town of Blue Ridge Summit, Pennsylvania, 'Raven Rock' or 'Site R'; Warrenton, North Virginia; Bear Wallow Road on Viewtree Mountain, and one on Rt. 802, Virginia; in the foothills of the Manzano Road Mountains, near Albuquerque, New Mexico; Atchison, Kansas; Amherst, Massachusetts; Napa, California; near Oakville, Sugar Grove, West Virginia; Ft. Belvoir, Virginia; West Point, New York; Groom Lake or Area S-4 near Nellis Air Force Base, Nevada; in the national forests in the Rocky Mountains of southwest Montana; Fort Meade, Maryland; Mount Pony, east of Culpepper, Virginia; on Riggs Road, off of Rt. 108, between Beetle Creek [Battle Creek?], Michigan; Denton, Texas; Bothell, Washington; Round Hill, Virginia; Emmitsbury, Maryland; Charlottesville, Virginia; Cheyenne Mountain, Colorado; Boston, Massachusetts; Olney, Maryland; Atlanta, Georgia; Chicago, Illinois; Kansas City, Missouri; Presidio, California; Fort Custer, Michigan; Richmond, Kentucky; Forest Park, Georgia; Palo Alto, Texas..."

We have also received reports that many small holding areas are being contructed at various locations around the nation. These are nothing more elaborate than fenced-in open fields of between 100 and 200 acres in uninhabited areas. Airline pilots have reported the appearance of these alleged detainment locations at numerous sites in the United States, including in western mountainous areas. These areas sometimes lack any identification whatsoever, while at other times they have signs saying such things as "Keep Out, Zoo Annex." On-site observers have reported that the fences in these facilities are sometimes partially buried, presumably to make escape from the areas more difficult.

One site near Topeka, Kansas covers 80 acres and bears a sign stating "Zoo Annex." Local citizens investigating the area have found that it is controlled by the Department of Corrections. Another camp has been stated to exist near Marseilles, Illinois. There is a 300' by 300' area is enclosed by fences and barbed wire, and an observation tower is located at each of the four corners of the facility. There is a reservoir connected to the camp, and fences inside break the facility into smaller yards. Observers suggest that it is large enough to hold 1400 detainees.

A letter to the editor in the July 1994 *Patriot Report* discusses the location of a detainment facility in Winnemucca, Nevada, which I have had verified by other sources:

"Gentlemen: Are you aware of the apparent detainment or concentration camp put up by the government 2 years ago on 1-80, mile marker 112, near Winnemucca, Nevada? This is on the south side of the road about 3/4 of a mile off the highway. I have not personally seen it, but several of my friends have. They say it appears to be able to hold around 5,000 people and is empty at this time. There are possibly three others sites in Nevada that have troops in them — one near Wells, 50-60 miles from Wendover toward Wells, one about 10 miles from Elko, one between Winnemucca and Wells, way out next to mountains — you can hardly see it."

From the *Intel Report* of the Militia of Montana, June 22, 1994 is a report dated June 15, 1994:

"Concerning unusual activity in Warren County, Pennsylvania and the northwestern portion of the Allegheny National Forest.

"A. Confirmed: large air strip (at least 500 yards wide), hangar and inaccessible (by road) area of western edge of Allegheny National Forest.

"B. Hiking trails, snowmobile trails, access roads, etc. in most of Allegheny National Forest were closed to the public this spring.

"C. Large portions of Allegheny National Forest fenced in with high chain link fence.

"D. Area within the Allegheny National Forest has been replanted. Sign states 'International Releafing Project.'

E. Treetop high towers have been erected in straight line from air strip from northeasterly direction. Towers extremely well lit up, very visible when lights are on.

"F. Reported, but unconfirmed that cameras and voice activated devices set up along some trails and roads in the Allegheny National Forest. (Note: The United States Forest Service has admitted to placing cameras in the forests in the northwestern part of the United States. Confirmed).

"G. An area of the National Forest is fenced in 'to control animal movement' by high chain link fence with barbed wire on top. Towers are in place outside the fenced area.

"H. Security was increased at large, local refinery (that is no longer owned by local people). The refinery supplies fuel to ships on St. Lawrence Seaway and Lake Erie, fuel to airports as far away as Rochester, New York, and gas to a large portion of the mid-Atlantic states and Ohio.

"I. This sleepy, little community (Warren, Pennsylvania) was infested with foreigners for about two weeks, earlier this year (Winter). Foreigners are very unusual in this community.

"J. Emergency Evacuation Program, in conjunction with FEMA, now in effect for entire county.

"K. Numerous sightings of black helicopters and military aircraft have been sighted in remote areas.

"L. Security at the local shopping mall has been increased. Mall now closes earlier and the doors are chained and padlocked, as well as being locked. (Note: It appears they are gearing up for civil unrest in this county and also the areas in the Allegheny National Forest that have been fenced in with towers could very well be a new holding facility for government dissenters)."

There are confirmed reports that massive new detention centers are being built in Ohio and Alabama for control by FEMA (Federal Emergency Management Agency), and that a huge FEMA prisoner transfer terminal is being constructed in Oklahoma City, Oklahoma. Mark Koernke reports that there is a detention camp readied at Indianapolis, Indiana, and that an aerial survey has been done of the multiple thousand-acre facility, including photos. The area is surrounded by a fence with barbed wire pointing inward, and includes a helicopter pad, large sewer treatment facilities, and rows of barracks. Signs on the center indicate only Blue Zone, Red Zone, and Green Zone.

I would be the first to admit that the locales of the concentration camps and holding facilities which I have listed above deserve further study. It is possible that there may be mistakes in identifying some of these locations, and some of these facilities may have been constructed for completely innocuous purposes of which we are unaware. Some of them may even actually be "Zoo Annexes," for all I know. In this chapter I have included a complete list of all of the credible reports of detention facilities which I have obtained, but further research — verifying or discrediting each of these sites as locations for concentration camps — should certainly be done by interested researchers.

Whether or not all of these facilities are intended to be used as detainment camps for U.S. citizens, it is obvious that they could be used for such a purpose, and that the government is not ruling out such a possibility. Proof of such a wild allegation? Try the Army field manual FM-10, "Civil Affairs Operation."

This Army manual states that one of the purposes of Army Civil Affairs is "Item 4. Assumption of full or partial executive, legislative and judicial authority over a country or area." This is said to include: "small towns and rural areas, municipalities of various population sizes, districts, counties, provinces or states, regions of national government."

In the study outline of the manual, on page j-24, listed under the heading "Penal Institutions 1-B," there are a number of entries under the designations of "concentration camps" and "labor camps," while on page d-4 is a receipt for seized property. This sample receipt is in English.

Every military commander and every grunt in the field may not be aware of the Orwellian plans which their government has carefully put in place, but it is obvious that those plans have been created. Whether concentration camps are used to incarcerate rioters during the course of urban insurrection, or protesters when the government finally shovels under the Constitution and the Bill of Rights hardly matters. The camps are there, at least in many of these locations, and if the government sees fit, they will be used.

Let me take a moment to further consider these reports of concentration camps on American soil. I differ from many anti-authoritarians, anti-New World Order types, and conspiracy theorists in my analysis of what purpose these facilities are intended for. The fact is, I don't believe that the government is likely to lock everyone up in one big, wholesale roundup. Many individuals in the political research community are, in fact, saying just this sort of thing. My guess is that it is more likely that the concentration camps are being set up to hold a select group of citizens. This group might include prison overflow, unbending patriots, random dissidents, anti-New World Order loudmouths, and the politically incorrect, but most particularly, I would think, groups and individuals who are not willing to go along with the next "baby step" of totalitarian control in the United States. Those would be the individuals who will not be willing to surrender their guns when the legislation inevitably comes down that outlaws their possession.

The reason I believe that the commitment of the entire populace of the U.S. to prison camps is not the likely scenario, is that we are already incarcerated in one of the most devilishly effective concentration camps ever devised: a "free" society (so the slavish and enslaving media tells us), in which all of the institutions are controlled by small cliques of monied elite. This elite is composed of the financial controllers of the world, the Rockefellers, the Rothschilds, and their ilk, along with their allied social stratum. There are no shortage of books which can be studied to get an in-depth understanding of this club of bloody-handed blue bloods. It has been estimated that 80% of our income is consumed in taxes, licenses, and increased prices due to taxes, licenses and other controls levied on business. How much more effective could the vampiric controllers' policies be?

Simply put, I just don't believe that it would be cost effective for the government to lock everybody up. I think they would rather have us slaving away at our two and three crummy jobs, drinking our beers and watching football on our days off, while they suck us dry with taxes and exorbitant prices. Certainly, the system can be fine-tuned so that tax resisters, gun hoarders, protesters, and whistle-blowers are located and taught the error of their ways, but I simply do not see any advantages for the controllers in putting the whole of America behind bars. Then the government would have to pay our room and board, and I doubt that is something that they want to do.

In my opinion the crunch is certainly coming — and coming soon — including the total confiscation of guns from the populace, and the revoking of privileges which we have gotten so used to that we don't even notice them, possibly including the freedom of speech, of assembly, of religion, of movement. At this moment those freedoms have been so abridged and selectively violated that their complete revocation is only a matter of degree. But I believe that it is only those who resist and speak out against this authoritarian takeover who will be spending their days in the camps. Who knows, though? I could be wrong.

4

National Emergency By Whose Definition?

The Constitution of the United States is meant to provide a bulwark against tyrannical assaults on the American public by its own government, but the Constitution has over the years been repeatedly violated and sidestepped to provide the controllers almost all the power they crave. One manner in which the Constitution has been compromised has been the declaration of a continual state of emergency in this country by succeeding presidents, a condition which has been in force without exception for over 40 years.

The "Special Committee on the Termination of the National Emergency" in 1973 provided two studies to Congress detailing this "continuing emergency." They stated that, "...the people of the U.S. have lived all of their lives under emergency rule. For 40 years, freedoms and governmental procedures guaranteed by the Constitution have been abridged by laws brought into force by states of national emergency."

Senator Church of Idaho commented on this incredible state of affairs, saying that, "...since 1933 it has been Congress' habit to delegate extensive emergency authority and not to set a terminating date. Consequently, the U.S. now has on the books at least 470 significant emergency powers statutes without time limitations. These statutes delegate to the President extensive discretionary powers... which affect the lives of American citizens in a host of all-encompassing ways. This vast range of powers, taken together, confer enough authority to rule this country without reference to normal constitutional processes. These emergency powers statutes are invoked by a Presidential declaration of a state of national emergency. The U.S. has been in such a state of declared national emergency since March 9, 1933. In addition to the national emergency declared by Roosevelt, there is also the national emergency proclaimed by Truman on December 16, 1950, plus Nixon's declarations on March 23, 1970 and August 15, 1971."

The Special Committee's report additionally noted that:

"At the end of the Korean war the official state of emergency was not terminated. It has not yet terminated... In this, what is for all practical purposes, permanent state of emergency. Over the course of at least 40 years, Presidents have had available an enormous, seemingly expanding and never-ending range of emergency powers... These prerogative powers appear to be virtually unlimited.... Because Congress and the public are unaware of the extent of emergency powers, there has never been any notable congressional or public objection made to this state of affairs. Nor have the courts imposed significant limitations. Since 1933 Congress has passed or recodified over 470 significant statutes delegating to the President powers that had been the prerogative and responsibility of the Congress since the beginning of the Republic... few if any foresaw that the temporary states of emergency declared in 1933, 1950, 1970, and 1971 would become what are now regarded collectively as virtually permanent states of emergency. Forty years can, in no way, be defined as a temporary emergency. In the view of the Special Committee, an emergency does not now exist. Congress, therefore, should act in the near future to terminate officially the states of national emergency now in effect."*(Congressional Record* — Senate, vol. 119 part 29, 93rd Congress, 1st session, November 19, 1973).

Such were the recommendations of the committee, although congressional representatives did not fall all over themselves to act on them. Indeed, since the issuing of that report American presidents have continued to enact additional Emergency Orders, providing themselves and their successors with virtually unlimited emergency powers. Remember, the "emergency" never ends, and has not since 1933.

What must be made clear is that Executive Orders and Presidential Directives are scrawled by Presidents of the United States without benefit of review of the people or Congress. This allows Presidents to unlawfully delegate to themselves powers which the Constitution rightfully denies, on the pretext that there is an "emergency" taking place which they need to respond to. Here are examples of some of the Executive Orders which are currently in place, and which the President can employ any time an event takes place which can be characterized as a national emergency (and the definition of what constitutes an emergency is purposefully and absolutely vague):

-EO 10995, authorizing the suspension of the freedom of speech and the commandeering of all communication media.

-EO 10997, authorizing the takeover of electrical systems and other fuel sources.

-EO 10998, providing for the government control of food sources, including farms.

-EO 10999, which authorizes the control or confiscation of the nation's transportation sources, public and private.

-EO 11000, which gives the government the right to form work brigades of citizens.

-EO 11001, providing for the takeover of all health, education, and welfare functions and facilities.

-EO 11002, authorizing a national registering of the populace.

-EO 11003, authorizing the takeover of all airplanes and airports.

-EO 11004, which gives government the mandate to relocate populations from one area to another.

-EO 11005, which provides for the government to take over railways, waterways, and public storage facilities.

-EO 12148, authorizing the Federal Emergency Management Agency to take over the executive functions of the government.

With the above Executive Orders ready to be activated virtually at a whim, there are no longer any barriers to a total dictatorship in the United States — except, perhaps, that small percentage of the populace who are informed, and an armed populace who know a police state when they see one. But don't wait for Ted Koppel to clue you in about any of this on his nightly report.

Russian Mi-24/HIND Attack Chopper as seen in Phoenix, Arizona in 1994

Armaments of the Apache AH-64 Black Chopper

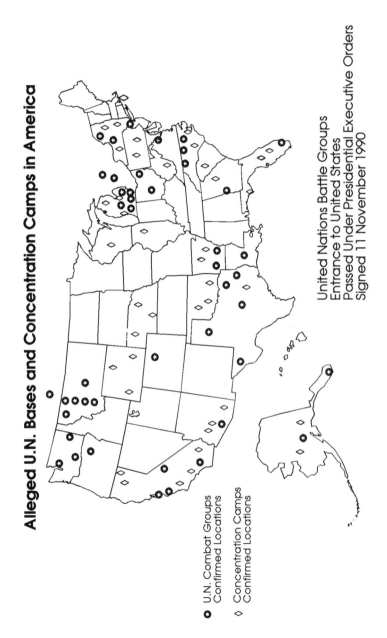

Alleged U.N. Bases and Concentration Camps in America

- ◉ U.N. Combat Groups
  Confirmed Locations
- ◇ Concentration Camps
  Confirmed Locations

United Nations Battle Groups
Entrance to United States
Passed Under Presidential Executive Orders
Signed 11 November 1990

Helicopters Part Of Training Exercise

The thundering sound of UH-1 and CH-46 military helicopters broke the noonday routine last Wednesday as the U. S. Marines Corps conducted urban drills over DeKalb County. Marine helicopters took off from Dobbins Air Force Base on their way to a simulated hostage situation at a vacant motel near I-20 and Candler Road. The Marines and helicopters are based at Camp Lejeune, and New River Air Station in North Carolina.

Jim Cook Jr. /Staff

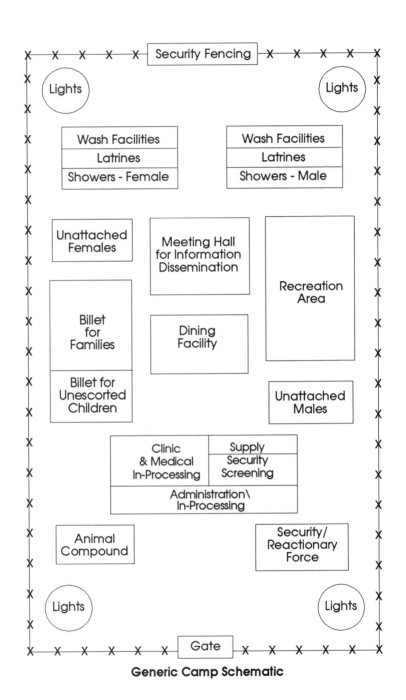

Generic Camp Schematic

Heavily armed assault and gunship helicopter, the Mi-24, code-named Hind, is in service in very large numbers in the Soviet Union.

TEN STANDARD FEDERAL REGIONS

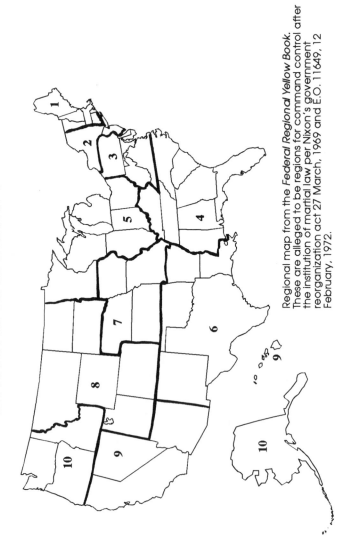

Regional map from the *Federal Regional Yellow Book*. These are alleged to be regions for command control after the institution of martial law per Nixon's government reorganization act 27 March, 1969 and E.O. 11649, 12 February, 1972.

5

FEMA

One of the responses to this bogus, continuing "emergency" enacted by unconstitutional Executive Order is the earlier-mentioned FEMA, the Federal Emergency Management Agency. This monstrosity of a government agency was birthed, like Rex 84, as a glimmer in the eye of then-California Governor Ronald Reagan in that halcyon year of 1969. That was when Reagan inaugurated a plan to train community leaders and others in the imperial favor in techniques for handling an unruly populace, many of whom had long hair and beards. This training consisted of a special program which was run at the National Guard Camp in San Luis Obispo, California. These cops and politicos were ushered through a regimen wherein a fictional town, "San Luisa," — note the similarity to the name of the town the program was held in — was partitioned into income and ethnic zones, and plans were brainstormed for infiltration and zone control during times of crisis. Within ten years of the program's operation, 14,000 persons had completed this seminar in iron fisting.

FEMA was formally set in motion by Jimmy Carter via Executive Order 12148, the Federal Emergency Management Act. This act incorporated all previous Presidential Executive Orders pertaining to emergencies, and gave the President virtually unlimited power to act during anything that constituted an emergency, or that the public could be brainwashed to believe did. FEMA took over a number of other governmental agencies which had been concerned with emergency action, including the Federal Emergency Broadcast System, the Federal Disaster Assistance Administration, and a large number of others.

FEMA is intended to assume the powers of government during "emergencies," even to the extent of taking over the powers of the President, if the situation is believed to warrant it. The organization is located in the top secret National Security Agency facility in Fort Meade, Maryland. In its more benign aspects, FEMA is seen as an "umbrella" agency that, during times of disaster or natural cataclysm, will step in to throw the stricken populace life preservers. But there are aspects of FEMA which have some worried, one being that only a small percentage, less than 10% of FEMA employees according to a Congressional investigation, is engaged in anything having to do with disaster relief. So what the hell is FEMA doing behind those closed doors at Fort Meade? Among other things, the agency is engaged in compiling computer records on millions of Americans, to provide a database for CAPS, Crisis Action Programs, to be deployed whenever the non-elected bureaucrats of FEMA anticipate something which might compromise almighty COG, what they term the "Continuity of Government."

Clarifying the kind of situations in which FEMA intervention might take place, in 1989 President Bush visited Cartagena, Columbia, for a drug summit attended by three Latin American Presidents. Rumors of a possible assassination attempt on Bush were passed on to FEMA officials who in turn hammered out an emergency program to be instituted in the event that a Stinger missile wielded by Juan Valdez turned Air Force 1 into a thousand points of light. FEMA came up with a plan to, if needed, round up and place into detention centers 10,000 Americans who had been singled out in their computer files as "activists, supporters, or sympathizers of terrorism in the United States," a definition broad enough to possibly include me and thee. FEMA performed the same sort of function during the Iraqi war (described by George Bush as "a major stepping stone to the New World Order"), setting into motion the means to incarcerate the persons on this same computerized list of "activists," while dutifully updating the list with thousands of additional names.

An excellent investigative report by *The Spotlight* (a newspaper perennially and unjustly smeared as "neo-Nazi" by the establishment press, and shunned by the liberal intelligentsia) has uncovered a new "national communications center" which FEMA is putting together in Salt Lake City. On site investigators report chain link and barbed wire fencing off a portion of the Salt Lake City airport, with National Guard tanks positioned in defensive locations. What seem to be laser sensors are placed on the fences, and signs warn that the area is off limits and that anyone making maps, photos, or drawings of the area is in violation of the National Security Act of 1950. Beyond the fence there is a helicopter ramp where "at least two, and probably four" Army Apache choppers (apparently fitted with rocket pods) are parked. At other positions in the compound satellite dishes cock their ears to the sky, apparently to facilitate FEMA communications.

At another location in Salt Lake City, a hamburger processing plant is said to hide another secretive FEMA installation. Across from the airport facilities is a large facility of the UniSys corporation, a company which has reportedly been the recipient of multi-billions of dollars of FEMA contract money in exchange for state-of-the-art electronics and communications monitoring equipment. There are reports that this FEMA facility is being constructed in order to monitor 800 telephone numbers countrywide, with particular attention being paid to companies engaged in the sale of guns and ammunition. And all this time I could have sworn that the possession of guns was a Constitutional right...

The beat goes on. During the latter half of 1994, typically without consulting or informing the American public, President Bill Clinton signed off a "Notice of Extension" to an Executive Order which George Bush had put in place on May 30, 1992. The Bush Executive Order dealt with a "declared national emergency to deal with the unrest and extraordinary threat to national security, foreign policy and economy of the United States constituted by policies of the governments of Serbia and Montenegro."

While policies dealing with Serbia and Montenegro seemingly have little to do with black helicopters, concentration camps, and the repression of American citizens, Clinton's signing of this Executive Order comprises a ploy which is by now a tad threadbare. By declaring that Bush's Executive Order is still in force, Clinton activates a host of Executive Orders enacted by other Presidents, and provides himself the opportunity to employ them at his somewhat compromised discretion. Given the latitude of interpretation available in the wording of those mealy-mouthed EOs, the possibilities for unconstitutional, tyrannical control of the nation become virtually astronomical in number. And some might say inevitable.

One tactic for a dictatorial takeover, an "emergency" which could be used to justify country-wide martial law, the trashing of constitutional rights, and the confiscation of all guns, would be to summon forth the hoary War on Drugs and the Drug and Crime Emergency Act. Backed up by an American news media conspiratorial to its core, the President could fan the flames of public hysteria and take full control over the United States with a well-placed televised fireside chat. Martial law would be declared, and suddenly we would be living in the kind of world we have only seen in Russia or the third world, a place where the populace have no rights whatsoever, and where the President can reshape the nation according to any Fabian-bred dystopian plans his wife pleases.

If you look around and carefully tippy-toe beyond the pabulum that the mainstream media offers you on the nightly news and in McPaper, there is no escaping the simple realization. The wolves are administrating the chicken coop. Barbecue never goes out of season.

6

The National Police Force

Get ready for the real 1984, *Brave New World*, and *Alternative 3*, all rolled up in one neat time bomb.

First a bit of perspective. On December 30, 1975 an announcement was issued by the California National Guard stating that they were prepared to provide emergency assistance to the populace in virtually any disaster situation which might arise, and would provide backup to the local police of Anytown, U.S.A. during emergency situations. Portions of this National Guard emergency preparedness plan were detailed in a briefing supplied to the Marine Corp Supply Center. The briefing stated that, "Under the Constitution and the laws of the United States, the preservation of law and order is the responsibility of local and state government. And the authority to maintain the peace and enforce the law is invested in the authorities of those governments." This briefing also brought up in passing something called "Garden Plot Forces" but did not elaborate on what those might be.

This Guard announcement came during a period in which military surveillance on the public was vastly increased. The military, in fact, was amassing more data on the populace than any other agency of the government at the time. During the late 1970s the Army began what might be considered a full-blown covert war against the American people, involving the CONUS and CONARC intelligence commands. These groups were reorganized as USAINTC, the Directorate of Civil Disturbance Planning, and the Division of Military Support. They hatched a myriad of secret operations with code names like GARDEN PLOT, GRAM METRIC, QUIET TOWN, LANTERN SPIKE, and PUNCH BLOCK, and part of their activities included compiling huge computerized databases of daily, weekly, and monthly intelligence on what the public was up to.

Robert E. Jordan III, general counsel to the Army, summed up the situation nicely: "The people on the other side were essentially the enemy. The army conducted a de facto war against all citizen protest, legitimate and illegitimate, violent and peaceful, white and black."

GARDEN PLOT was the key plan to be used by the Army, the National Guard, and civilian forces in the event of civil disruption. GARDEN PLOT readied military and local leaders for no-holds-barred combat with the people of the United States and brainstormed the logistics of these operations in "war room" surroundings. Twenty-four hour situational monitoring country-wide and a central Dr. Strangelovian "domestic war room" were important parts of the GARDEN PLOT operation, and were maintained in complete secrecy from the public, causing me to idly wonder what sort of "wars" the government is currently cooking up against we the people.

As early as 1962 J. Edgar Hoover had provided total access to the massive files of the FBI to the military, in exchange for riot-control seminars which the Army gave to members of the FBI on a bi-annual basis.

Shortly thereafter there was an article in the San Gabriel Valley Tribune where plans to implement a national police force were discussed. It was revealed that the major powers behind this push consisted of the LEAA (Law Enforcement Assistence Administration, funded by the Department of Justice) and the Police Foundations (with funding coming from the pro-New World Order Ford Foundation), although both groups characterize their purpose to be that of lending a helping hand to local agencies.

To get an idea of the outlook of these groups, we may quote Patrick Murphy, the administrator of the Police Foundations, who has stated, "I have no fear of a national police force. Our 40,000 police departments are not sacred."

The LEAA, significantly, is connected to the United Nations, and provides funding for the United Nations Clearinghouse, in Rome, Italy. One of the functions of that organization is to exchange American police information with the cops in Russia. I suspect that this would have seemed a somewhat radical program to the average American in the mid-1970s.

The program that the LEAA and the Police Foundations formulated was titled (and perhaps still is) Operation Cable Splicer, a portion of the previously mentioned Operation GARDEN PLOT martial law program. Cable Splicer was delivered as a training course in most states, with participants drawn from the military, the police, and the military reserve. Cable Splicer training was delivered under the innocuous title of "Civil Emergency Management Course" and the Cable Splicer program, according to Dr. William R. Pabst in his article "A National Emergency: Total Takeover," was:

"A) Keep the people from gathering in the streets.

"B) Isolate and neutralize the revolution's leadership.

"C) Dispersal of crowds and demonstrators.

"This is followed by successful prosecution in order to: 1) Validate the action of the police; 2) Deny the arrestees propaganda materials, and; 3) Deny them the opportunity to recover money damages against the police for arresting them."

The following scenario of civil disruption — which would be considered highly paranoid if it had been suggested by anyone but the cops — is quoted from Cable Splicer materials:

"Phase One — an arrest and shooting provoke crowd unrest and threats against public officials and a riot begins to form.

"Phase Two — police vehicles are ambushed, various attempted assassinations of public officials occur, destruction and raiding of armories occur, and thousands of people begin to gather and local police lose control.

"Phase Three - increased movement of rioters and the crowds must be dispersed before they become sympathetic with the rioters. The National Guard and the local police lose control."

During one Cable Splicer conference, the Deputy Attorney General of California commented that any individual who goes against the policies of the State, even in verbal fashion, is an enemy to the people. He was not the only one during the same time period advocating such "radical" ideas. *The Oakland Tribune* in 1976 provided a good look into Cable Splicer:

"Last Saturday the California National Guard unveiled a new Law Enforcement Assistance Force — LEAF, a specially trained and outfitted Military Police unit, whose members will serve as shock-troops in the state's war against political protesters and demonstrators.

"I saw a full-dress exhibition of what the California National Guard has planned for the next American revolution. Helicopters, SWAT teams, civilian military policemen in jack boots and helmets, twelve-gauge shotguns, .38 and .45 caliber pistols, radios, walkie talkies, and electrically-controlled intelligence centers wired for instant communications with any police force in the state.

"LEAF is a 1,000 member unit put together this year to handle unique law enforcement problems such as mass civil disobedience, protest demonstrations and riots. In other words, breaking heads and taking names. LEAF has the support of Governor Brown, a quarter-million dollars worth of grants from the federal government, and no public opposition from civil liberties groups.

"For all its ineptitude however, LEAF has a frightening possibility from a civil liberty standpoint. It is a direct product of the California Cable Splicer conferences — a series of high-level secret meetings between government officials, law enforcement officers and military planners held during the late '60s and early '70s. The meetings were held as late as 1975 so far, as many public records show. These were the conferences which Counter-Spy magazine had identified as California's 'Garden Plot subplan.'

"Gary Davis — Governor Brown's right hand man — says LEAF is to assist civil police, not to replace them. Gary says, 'Civilians could expect a civilian type law enforcement rather than what is commonly known as Martial Law.' Despite this assurance, LEAF's exercises look disturbingly like the military coup described in the novel, *Seven Days In May*.

"LEAF soldiers with nightsticks stood at intersections, stopping cars with suspicious occupants, checking I.D. cards and generally intimidating onlookers with their SWAT style uniforms, their sidearms and helmets. Perhaps more ominously, several participants in the role-playing exercises Saturday admitted that even under simulated pressure there have already been a number of incidents where the LEAF troops used excessive force to quell disturbances — even though their orders forbade it."

Operation Cable Splicer was no poorly funded Band-Aid of a project, either. The LEAA received over a billion dollars in funding during the period in which Cable Splicer was in operation.

Brigadier General J.L. Julenic, senior Army officer of the Pentagon National Guard Bureau, admitted to the scale of the operation: "I know of no state that did not have some form of these exercises within the last year."

William Pabst had access to the material contained in the Cable Splicer manual, consisting of six loose-leaf binders:
"On page 4, paragraph 10 on Public Information, the instructions state: 'As a means to prevent adverse publicity or misleading psychological effects in regard to coordinating, planning, and conducting this exercise, all military participants involved will perform such duties in civilian clothing when exercise oriented activities are conducted at law enforcement facilities. In the event inquiries are received regarding this exercise, the response should be limited to identifying the activity as a continuous, joint law enforcement-military liaison effort and a continuation of coordination established last year.' On page 6, security guidance is explained to the effect that if anybody asks any questions, limit the information that is given out on the basis of it being in the interest of 'national interest.'

"The manual includes instructions on operation of confinement facilities, handling and processing prisoners — including searching, transporting, feeding, housing and handling of the special class of persons called 'detainees.' The plan also specifically includes a proposition for confiscation of privately-owned weapons and ammunition."

After the completion of the Cable Splicer exercise, General Stanley R. Larsen, the commanding general of the Sixth Army, put everything in perspective:
"The most serious challenge facing all of us will be the challenge of discharging our legitimate responsibilities. For a significant portion of a society at large is likely to regard us with suspicion and to question, even challenge our authority on the basic assumption of our profession. Part of this challenge we must be prepared to deal with; a potentially dangerous portion of our society which, in truth, could well become the domestic enemy."

By 1989 the mood of the country had changed, or at least the government thought that it had, and so they were a little more forthcoming in letting their plans be known. Now a Fabian could freely be a Fabian, and one of Heather's Two Mommies might even be the Attorney General.

By this time, according to the *Washington Post* of July 15th, 1994, the Clinton administration was "seeking congressional authorization for U.S. spies to continue conducting clandestine searches at foreign embassies in Washington and other cities without a federal court order." Part of their plan was that government operatives would also be able to search without warrant the homes of individuals — American citizens — merely suspected of participating in activities which compromised national security.

Sans fanfare, in 1989 the federal government passed laws in all of the states authorizing the use of government funds for the creation of a "National Police Force," so-called by Clinton and Gore in their book *Putting People First*. This Frankenstein monster of a police force is currently being stitched together by placing local and state forces under a single national directorate, with an intended total force of 100,000 federal agents, a figure rendered more impressive by the realization that other agencies including the BATF, DEA, CIA, the FBI and any number of other goon squads can be utilized simultaneously with this National Police Force. Thus Clinton and his successors will have at their beck two to three times the 100,000 person available manpower of the National Police Force. The National Police Force now exists in rudimentary form in almost all of the states, and its purpose is to provide an easily-utilized strike force for intervention on a local or national, rather than international level. One of the major elements of the National Police is what has been termed the Multi-Jurisdictional Task Force (the MJTF). We are told that the MJTF was conceived of by the Department of Defense and is coordinated jointly by FEMA and the National Guard Bureau. The MJTF incorporates under a single arm patch members from a number of different governmental agencies (including the BATF, the FDA, the CIA, the DEA, the IRS, Federal Marshalls, the National Guard, and local police personnel) as well as civilian forces, and during what is designated as a national emergency the MJTF may also call up draftees. One of the more controversial allegations about the MJTF is that they will use street gangs and Guardian Angels as "shock troops" when performing search and seizure on Americans. Mark Koernke, in the video *America In Peril,* warns us that, "If anybody has listened to *National Public Radio,* you will note that on several different occasions, one of which being in October 1992, it was announced (during a one hour program) that there was an idea around to convert the street gangs to 'law enforcement' personnel. Through these activities, a truce was signed by most of the large gangs in the city of Los Angeles. At the time, there were negotiations in progress in Chicago and New York with the gangs. Since that initial action, a full agreement has been made in Los Angeles. Both the 'Crips' and the 'Bloods' are being trained, equipped, and provided uniforms with federal funding through the State of California. Chicago has recently finalized an agreement with their gangs. The civilian gangs will be the 'master forces' (being expendable) to first come through your door."

We do know that included among the manpower which the MJTF may utilize are the state defense forces of "civilian soldiers" which operate in at least 25 states (although it is said that at least three such forces have been dismantled, due to demands made by the public, law enforcement officials, or by the press). These state defense forces consist primarily at this time of individuals intended to be MJTF officers, and they continue to drill in order to acquire the skills necessary to "prevent or suppress subversive activity." Judging from the reports we have seen, the duties of these officers might be to command forces who would search private dwellings, interrogate the population, and transport designated individuals to concentration camp-style facilities.

These duties might be identical to those employed in a staging for "urban warfare" set up in three Chicago neighborhoods and, again, described by Mark Koernke: "The units that were brought in were trained in house-to-house search and how to secure a neighborhood. They then attacked a second neighborhood, secured it, and learned how to secure the two neighborhoods while going on to take a third. After the group that was being trained had gone through this attack-and-secure mechanism, they were transferred to different parts of Cleveland where they were actually deployed against the population."

Koernke has also provided intelligence relating to incidents in which urban search and seizures operations directed against firearms have taken place, although these kinds of interventions are only infrequently noted in the mainstream press when they happen. Koernke notes that, beginning in late 1992, a number of unconstitutional invasions of American cities have taken place, including Operation Clean Sweep in Chicago, where black helicopters were employed and troops went door-to-door, breaking into houses and confiscating guns and ammunition. Operation Achilles in Cleveland, Ohio, utilized FINCEN and MJTF troops, as well as the Ohio Guard. In Cleveland the operation actually was covered on *National Public Radio*.

One group under MJTF command and conceived to deal with threats posed by the American public, as opposed to foreign threats, is the California State Military Reserve. In the event that the National Guard was not available, this MJTF unit would be summoned, and would be used to coordinate the formation of a military force composed of rapidly-drafted Americans without qualms about using automatic rifles and riot batons against other Americans. Eight hundred officers belonging to this MJTF force would provide the basis for running the entire force in California, although it is said that plans are afoot for roughly doubling the numbers of these officers-in-training. Based upon the State Military Reserve Mobilization Plan, when the militia is called up in California these officers will in charge of training recruits at Camp San Luis Obispo, where the recruits will be issued M-14 automatic rifles, .45 caliber sidearms, and riot gear. Captain Richard Grossman participated in one training exercise and described his qualifications for training MJTF troops: "As the weapons instructor in the police department, I'm also assigned as a SWAT [Special Weapons and Tactics] team member... I've been to basic SWAT course, I've been to sniper SWAT courses... all the various SWAT courses, and of course, SWAT teams are trained in riot control. I've attended most of the civilian riot-control, civil disturbance and firearms-instructor courses that are given in the state of California."

A significant aspect of these state militias which they are not anxious to discuss is that of intelligence gathering. The report for the 1989 State Military Reserve Mobilization mentions one of the functions of the Reserve is to create and maintain intelligence and counterintelligence files on the populace.

During the last two years we have been receiving numerous verified reports of foreign military forces training in the U.S., and it is probable that at least some of these troops are part of joint MJTF-U.N. exercises. These groups are said to be made up of primarily European extraction, including French, German, Dutch and Belgian troops. There is also supposed to be a Nepalese Gurkha contingent of U.N. soldiers currently in training in Montana near the border of Canada, along with the U.S. 197th Mechanized Infantry, two British brigades, the Ist Canadian Armored Division, and a brigade of Belgian soldiers.

The machinations of the cop-happy controllers seem to never end. Bill Clinton stated in April of 1994 that he plans to merge the U.S. military with civilian police forces, ostensibly to provide citizen accountability for the military, but in actual fact opening wide the door to the unconstitutional practice of allowing the U.S. military to police American soil.

7

New World Armies

I have bantered about the term *New World Order* in this book, assuming that most everyone would know what I was talking about. What, however, is the precise definition of the phrase?

Author Lindsey Williams provided perhaps the most authoritative information during an interview on the Jim French Show, on KIRO radio, Seattle, Washington, on October 2, 1991.

Williams: "There's a new expression that's very common now, heard quite often [from] our President, entitled *New World Order*, and no one ever seems to know the definition to it."

French: "Do you have a definition of it? Is there an official definition of it? When George Bush says *New World Order*, what does he mean?"

Williams: "Well, there was some very close friends of President Bush who met in Germany recently at what was dubbed as the Brandt Commission; it was also called the Fifth Socialist International. A very prestigious group of people, and at their meeting they formally adopted a definition of the expression New World Order. Just a few individuals who were there... Former World Bank President, Robert McNamara was there, who by the way is a personal friend of President Bush; former Secretary of Commerce, Peter Peterson was present; none other than

Newsweek magazine's owner and editor, Katherine Graham, was there, just to name a few of the very prestigious individuals who were there."

French: "This is the 'Brandt Commission?'"

Williams: "Brandt Commission. I don't know why they called it the Fifth Socialist International, or why they called it Brandt Commission. All I know is that they met in West Germany, and in the course of their meeting they officially adopted a definition of the expression New World Order, and all of these individuals approved it, and signed it, saying that they officially adopted this as the definition... of the expression that's being used by our President and Mr. Gorbachev, and Mr. Yeltsin..."

French: "So, what is their definition?"

Williams: "I will read it: 'A supra-national authority to regulate world commerce and industry; an international organization that would control the production and consumption of oil; an international currency that would replace the dollar; a world development fund that would make funds available to free and Communist nations alike; an international police force to enforce the edicts of the New World Order.'"

French: "What are you reading that from?"

Williams: "This was published in the *McAlvaney Intelligence Advisory* and Don McAlvaney produces one of the most respected financial newsletters in the world today. He got it right from the minutes of the Brandt Commission when they met in West Germany in February of Nineteen and Ninety-one."

Obviously, the term "New World Order" is not quite the catch-phrase loosely signifying "world cooperation" which the internationalists would like us to believe. In actual fact, the New World Order is simply the long term game plan of the Fabians and other communists, plans which were most clearly elucidated in Fabian H.G. Wells' non-fiction books, such as *The New World*

Order and *The Open Conspiracy*. Why not let the Soviet Union dissolve, the New World Orderlies must be saying, if the United States and the rest of the planet is recreated in its image?

We can see precursors of current New World Order policies in the "Military Government Reserve Units" of 1951-52, described in the 1955 book by Dr. V. Orval Watts, *The United Nations: Planned Tyranny*. Watts explained that,

"At Fort MacArthur, California, and in other centers, considerable numbers of American military forces went into training in 1951 as Military Government Reserve Units. What they were for may appear from their practice maneuvers during the two years 1951-1952.

"Their first sally took place on July 31, 1951, when they simulated an invasion and seizure of nine California cities: Compton, Culver City, Inglewood, Hawthorne, Huntington Park, Long Beach, Redondo Beach, South Gate and Torrance. The invading forces, however, did not fly the American flag. They came in under the flag of the United Nations, and their officers stated that they represented the United Nations.

"These forces arrested the mayors and police chiefs, and pictures later appeared in the newspapers showing these men in jail. The officers issued manifestos reading by virtue of the authority vested in me by the United Nations Security Council. At Huntington Park they held a flag-raising ceremony, taking down the American Flag and running up in its place the United Nations banner.

"On April 3, 1952, other units did the same thing at Lampasas, Texas. They took over the town, closed churches, strutted their authority over the teachers and posted guards in classrooms, set up concentration camps, and interned businessmen after holding brief one-sided trials without habeas corpus.

"Said a newspaper report of that Texas invasion: "But the staged action almost became actual drama when one student and two troopers forgot it was only make-believe. 'Ain't nobody going to make me get up,' cried John Snell, 17, his face beet-red. One of the paratroopers shoved the butt of his rifle within inches of Snell's face and snarled, 'You want this butt placed in your teeth? Get up!'"

"The invaders put up posters listing many offenses for which citizens would be punished. One of them read: 'Publishing or circulating or having in his possession with intent to publish or circulate, any printed or written matter... hostile, detrimental, or disrespectful to the government of any other of the United Nations.'

"Think back to the freedom-of-speech clause of the United States Constitution which every American officer and official is sworn to support and defend. What was in the minds of those who prepared, approved and posted these U.N. proclamations?

"The third practice seizure under the United Nations flag occurred at Watertown, New York, August 20, 1952, more than a year later than the first ones. It followed the same pattern set in the earlier seizures in California and Texas. Is this a foretaste of World Government, which so many Americans seem to want?"

The stage was further set for the introduction of the New World Order by the Kennedy administration's "Freedom from War: The U.S. Program for General and Complete Disarmament in a Peaceful World" (Dept. of State publication 7277). On September 1, 1961, a courier from the U.S. State Department placed this document into the hands of the U.N. Secretary General, which outlined the steps to be taken to turn over the U.S. military to the U.N. The document suggested the means for "...progressive reduction of the war-making capability of the nations and the simultaneous strengthening of international institutions to settle disputes and maintain the peace..." I'm not even sure that the Birchers screamed.

With these officials of the State Department speaking for "The nations of the world" in this "Declaration on Disarmament," they presumed to "declare their goal to be the disbanding of all national armed forces and the prohibition of their re-establishment in any form whatsoever, other than those required to preserve internal order and for contributions to a United Nations Peace Force".

"The nations of the world," so the State Department professed to believe, wanted to get rid of all weapons including armaments capable of mass destruction, "other than those required for a United Nations Peace Force." Like Clinton, it wasn't that they minded guns, it was that they didn't like other people to have guns.

"The Nations of the world," the document stated, would also establish an organization enforcing compliance in disarmament, and a three part program that would disarm the United States and simultaneously arm the United Nations. Here is how this would come about:

"Stage One: "The states shall develop arrangements in Stage One for the establishment in Stage Two of a U.N. Peace Force."

Stage Two: "During Stage Two, states shall develop further peace-keeping process of the United Nations to the end that the United Nations can effectively in Stage Three deter or suppress any threat or use of force in violation of the purposes and principles of the United Nations."

Stage Three: "In Stage Three, progressive controlled disarmament and continuously developing principles and procedures of international law would proceed to a point where no state would have the military power to challenge the progressively strengthened U.N. Peace Force."

I would say that currently we are well into Stage Two.

At the same time that the State Department proposed its quiet but revolutionary castration of the American military, the Congress passed Public Law 87-297, "The Arms Control and Disarmament Act," dated September 26, 1961, which brought into being the United States Arms Control and Disarmament Agency. This agency was to be concerned with:

"The preparation for and management of United States participation in international negotiations in the arms control and disarmament field.

"The dissemination and coordination of public information concerning arms control and disarmament."

As well as, "The preparation for, operation of, or as appropriate, direction of United States participation in such control systems as may become part of United States control and disarmament activities."

"The so-called Disarmament Act," Congressman James B. Utt complained in the *Washington Report* for February 14, 1963, "Sets up a super-agency with power greater than the power of Congress, which delegated it. The law was almost a duplication, word for word, of a disarmament proposal by the Kremlin in 1959, and so we find ourselves again advancing the Moscow policy. As an example of the power, Section 43 (of the Disarmament Act) provided that the President may, in advance, exempt actions of the director (U.S. Disarmament Agency) from the provisions of law relating to contracts or expenditures of government funds whenever he determines that such action is essential in the interest of United States arms control and disarmament and security policy.

"The Disarmament legislation was passed for the purpose of implementing the Department of State Publication 7277, entitled *Freedom from War ---- The United States Program for General and Complete Disarmament in a Peaceful World.* This little gem from the State Department laid out the program for complete disarmament on a three stage basis, the purpose of which was to reduce the armaments of every nation to almost zero point, including our own National Guard, and to concurrently augment an international peace force under the benevolent guidance of the communist-dominated United Nations, whose recent, murderous actions in Katanga should make every American shudder at the thought of the U.N. blue helmets enforcing the edicts of U Thant in this Republic. The idea was to reduce our military capability to zero with the exception of a small federal army trained in counterinsurgency to put down civil strife within this country.

"One of the first steps of the Arms Control Agency was to recommend the repeal of the Connally Amendment and to make this country completely subservient to the International Court of Justice. The International Court of Justice is about as un-American as possible. It is true that the World Court is not supposed to act on domestic matters, but so does the U.N. charter provide that the U.N. should not inject itself into domestic matters. Yet the Congo is living proof that they have no intention of living by the charter. There is every intention on the part of the Disarmament Agency to destroy the sovereignty of this nation and put us under the control of international tyranny, and they are moving rapidly in this direction."

If there is any doubt about the plans of the U.N. to, quite literally, control the world, then here is a quick scan of Memorandum No. 7, "A World Effectively Controlled by the United Nations," by Lincoln P. Bloomfield, a member of that elitist propaganda bureau, the Council on Foreign Relations, and commissioned by the State Department in 1962. Bloomfield pontificated that:

"A world effectively controlled by the United Nations is one in which 'world government' would come about through the establishment of supranational institutions, characterized by mandatory universal membership and some ability to employ physical force. Effective control would thus entail a preponderance of political power in the hands of a supranational organization... The present U.N. Charter could theoretically be revised in order to erect such an organization equal to the task envisioned, thereby codifying a radical rearrangement of power in the world...

"The principal features of a model system would include the following: 1) power, sufficient to monitor and enforce disarmament, settle disputes, and keep the peace — including taxing powers; 2) an international police force balanced appropriately among ground, sea, air, and space elements, consisting of 500,000 men recruited individually, wearing a U.N. uniform, and controlling a nuclear force composed of 50-100 mixed land-based mobile missiles and undersea-based missiles, averaging one megaton per weapon; 3) a government divided among three branches; and 4) compulsory jurisdiction of the International Court."

Presently, the plans for the U.N. control of the world can be plainly read in "The Human Development Report 1994," released on June 1 by the United Nations Human Development Program. The UNHDP, interestingly enough, is headed by James Gustave Speth, who was project director for the infamous Global 2000 report of the Carter administration. This was the report that made the reduction of the world's population by 2 billion individuals by the year 2000 an avowed target of the U.S. government.

As remarkable as it may seem, the time table for the creation of the New World Order with the U.N. as the controlling body is intended to be implemented, according to the UNHDP, by March 1995. Replacing national security with the interests of the one world order, the UNHDP proposals include the following: the creation of a World Court, a World Police, A World Central Bank, World Treasury, a World Economic Security Council, and a World Trade and Production Organization (dictating production quotas to nations). The UNHDP report also calls for the implementation of numerous global taxes (including income tax, foreign exchange taxes, taxes on demilitarization savings, and pollution taxes).

The document also stipulates the increase of U.N. military powers and the organization's ability to intervene in territories unaligned to the purposes of the New World Order, while also dictating that military forces be stripped from developing countries. The document specifically lauds Oscar Arias, former President of Costa Rica, and his call for a U.N. Global Demilitarization Fund, which would provide funds to developing countries willing to disarm. This call for disarmament is backed up by the Economic Security Council, which uses disarmament as a prerequisite for monies provided to third world countries.

The UNHDP document also includes what some have called a "hit list" of developing countries, i.e. a list of countries which are in need of U.N. "pre-emptive action." On the list are Afghanistan, Angola, Haiti, Iraq, Mozambique, Suidan, Zaire, Burundi, Georgia, Liberia, Rwanda, and Tajikistan, while Brazil, South Africa, Egypt, Mexico, and Nigeria are noted as potential future hot spots requiring intervention.

The document makes plain the reason for the increase in U.N. powers, indicating that these powers will be used to enforce population reduction on otherwise reticent nations. The report, paralleling the earlier mentioned Global 2000 report, says that population must be stabilized at 7.3 billion persons, and backs up this quota with a proposal for annual economic and social reviews in which the politicos of each country are summoned to account for their progress in population reduction. Those not hitting quota, one presumes, will be liable to reduction of U.N. funding, or possible intervention by the U.N. Army.

No, this U.N. document is not merely idle blue-skying on the part of globalist desk jockeys. In the December 14, 1992 issue of *Time* magazine, Strobe Talbott of the Trilateral Commission, and second-in-command at the Clinton State Department, put a fine point on the matter: "Once a country utterly loses its ability to govern itself, it also loses its claim to sovereignty and should become a ward of the United Nations." Talbott is not one to hedge his words when it comes to the New World Order. In the same article, he stated, "I'll bet that within the next 100 years, nationhood as we know it will be obsolete; all states will recognize a single global authority. A phrase briefly fashionable in the mid-20th century — citizen of the world — will have assumed real meaning.... All countries are basically social arrangements. No matter how permanent and even sacred they may seem at any one time, in fact they are all artificial and temporary."

The U.N. is also deadly serious in its World Constitution, drafted in conjunction with the World Constitution and Parliament Association.

"The preamble to the World Constitution says in part: "Realizing that Humanity today has come to a turning point in history and that we are on the threshold of a new world order, which promises to usher in an era of peach, prosperity, justice and harmony;... Aware of the interdependence of people, nations and all of life;

"Aware that man's abuse of science and technology has brought Humanity to the brink of disaster, through the production of horrendous weaponry of mass destruction and to the brink of ecological and social catastrophe; ... Aware of the misery and conflicts caused by the ever increasing disparity between rich and poor; Conscious of our obligation to posterity to save Humanity from imminent and total annihilation;

"Conscious that Humanity is One, despite the existence of diverse nations, races, creeds, ideologies and cultures and that the principle of unity in diversity is the basis for a new age when war shall be outlawed and peace prevail: when the earth's total resources shall be equitably used for human welfare; and when basic human rights and responsibilities shall be shared by all without discrimination; Conscious of the inescapable reality that the greatest hope for survival of life on earth is the establishment of a democratic world government..."

Although I don't recall being asked to comment on the matter — do you? — the document says that, "We the citizens of the world, hereby resolve to establish a world federation to be governed in accordance with this Constitution, for the Federation of Earth."

Article III of the would-be World Constitution elaborates on the "Grant of Specific Powers to the World Government" and proposes that the world federation "Supervise disarmament and prevent re-armament; prohibit and eliminate the design, testing, manufacture, sale, purchase, and possession of weapons of mass destruction and all such weapons as the World Parliament may decide."

Suffice it to say that the World Constitution proposes that the world federation control everything, anyhow, anywhere, period. This includes transportation, immigration, trade, industry, labor supply, communications, banking, population growth, insurance, natural resources, education, currency, and anything which slipped their mind at the moment.

The World Constitution naturally includes the formation of a World Police Force "to handle intra-state violence or problems, should they occur."

While the World Constitution may not be slammed into law in a midnight session of Congress for at least a while, the U.N. is currently up-scaling its activities to reflect greatly magnified ambitions. The Secretary General's staff has now transformed from a small planning body into one of the most powerful nexuses of worldwide power, outclassing in available man and firepower the resources of most countries, and utilizing 82 general officers calling the shots on new U.N. incursions.

Currently, the United Nations is involved in at least 17 international interventions, with at least 73,000 U.N. soldiers on duty. In 1992 *The New York Times* printed a list of 48 countries where they believed U.N. interventions might take place in the future. Additional countries which might be targeted were added to this list by Gerald Helman and Steven Ratner in *Foreign Policy*, the magazine of the Council on Foreign Relations. Helman and Ratner wrung their hands about the foremost difficulty of U.N. interventionism being "the quaintly archaic notion of sovereignty." And that fairly sums up the attitude of these silver spoon-bred psychos, that the American populace's unwillingness to see themselves as simply another "resource" on the global plantation is "quaintly archaic."

Further plans of the U.N. were clarified at a recent meeting of the elitist Trilateral Commission, on April 12, 1993. At the Trilateral meeting, members President Clinton, Secretary of State Warren Christopher, and Treasury Secretary Lloyd Bentsen were handed an offer they couldn't refuse — not that there is any indication that they wanted to, you understand — creating further steppingstones to the final New World Order takeover. This plan featured the following stipulations for these American politicians to implement in the U.S.:

— The necessity for the ratification of the North American Free Trade Agreement (which later took place). Although it was admitted that U.S. jobs would be lost due to the migration of industry across the border to Mexico, this was seen as a necessity in the formation of the Western Hemisphere community, intended to be a single political entity much like a United Europe. It is not known whether job retraining in the usage of adobe is part of the NAFTA agreement, although current test results of public school students demonstrate that they are being ably trained for just these kinds of skills for the future global marketplace.

— The formation of a permanent standing army under the direction of the U.N., and the continuing ability of the U.N. to intervene in the affairs of nations, regardless of whether these nations wish the presence of the U.N. "peacekeeping force."

— The granting to the U.N. of the power to set immigration policies for its member countries, deemed an "international migration regime." A draft of the stipulations state that, "An international migration regime would include new legal instruments and the operational capacity to respond to the full range of international migration situations... A critical feature of such arrangements is that national decision authorities yield to international standards and scrutiny in their decision-making." America was criticized for its non-policy on immigration, and its lack of "multicultural programs." Apparently our wide-open borders with Mexico, and the transformation of Los Angeles into a suburb of Tijuana do not qualify as "multicultural programs."

At the Trilateral Commission meeting, John Roper, Director of the Western European Union and a former member of the British Parliament gave a talk heralding the formation of the New World Order and counseled, "The United Nations should have at its permanent disposal a highly trained, standing-ready force of some four or five battalions — each with some 600-700 troops — drawn from one or two nations and trained to operate as a single unit."

"At a second level, the United Nations should have rapid deployment forces from the armed forces of member states which could be deployed at a very few days' notice." Roper also suggested that smaller countries might pool their resources to create brigades of soldiers, while larger nations should each provide 5,000 men to the U.N. standing army. Roper sensibly cautioned that a larger commitment would be required for large military interventions.

Actually, Roper is being excessively modest about the planned size of the U.N. Army. Based upon classified documents of the U.N. Secretary General's staff which were acquired by *The Spotlight* newspaper, the U.N. world police will take the form of three units:

"A Rapid Response Peace Force some 60,000 strong, described as an interposition force capable of instant intervention in any trouble spot under direct command of the U.N. Security Council.

"A Permanent Peacekeeping Force, designated a conflict control corps, 275,000 strong, under command of officers from various nations appointed by the U.N. Military Staff committee.

"A Standing Reserve Peace Force numbering 500,000 troops as a standing military reserve of national components, designated, trained, equipped and earmarked for U.N. duty whenever required. Another participant in the Trilateral meeting, Enid C.B. Schoettle of the Council on Foreign Relations, echoed Roper's demand for larger U.N. forces, and suggested means of financing this kind of an arrangement, suggesting international taxes on international air travel, shipping, global traffic flows and the like."

Ugandan Olara Otunnu, the president of the International Peace Academy in New York, talked about the necessity for the U.N. army to be able invade countries at will, regardless of the wishes of the country. "There is a major evolution in thinking at the level of international public opinion," he stated, "that can no longer accept that massive and dramatic suffering should be shielded behind the walls of sovereignty... In effect, the notion of what constitute the 'domestic affairs' of a state is undergoing some change."

The ambitions of the U.N. and its controllers seem to be limitless, and of course parallel the ambitions of the current American administration. For one thing, the U.N. is just as interested in gun-grabbing as Bill Clinton is. Proof of this can be found in the U.N. document, "The Chairman's Working Paper on Guidelines for International Arms Transfers" (A/C-10/1994/W.III/CRP 2 Rev. 1).

This U.N. paper makes it clear that the policy makers in the group feel that they should have the ability to control guns —

virtually everything about guns — worldwide. The working paper proposes that, "Arms permitted (legally sold and licensed) for civilian use, whether imported or of domestic manufacture, should also be subject to controls at all points, from production and acquisition up to the time they are sold to an individual (citizen)." If it is not obvious, what the New World Order is offering is world peace at the price of a total world dictatorship. Some see this as a reasonable exchange.

Possibly the most decisive — and scary — of President Clinton's recent actions ushering in the New World Order and U.N. world control was the signing of Presidential Decision Directive 25 (PDD-25) on May 3rd, 1994, an action which places U.S. military commanders under the jurisdiction of the United Nations during U.N.-controlled actions. Not surprisingly, the main text of the directive remains classified. In response to requests for a copy of the document, Anthony Lake, assistant to the President National Security Affairs, grudgingly released a 15-page "unclassified summary."

PDD-25 was originally written as Presidential Review Directive 13 (PDD-13), issued in 1993, which included a disclaimer penned by General Colin Powell, at the time the chairman of the Joints Chiefs of Staff. This disclaimer "allowed U.S. commanders under U.N. command to not comply with orders which they believe are: (1) outside the mandate of the mission, (2) illegal under U.S. law, or, (3) militarily imprudent or unsound." PDD-25 has had these exemptions removed. It is also important to note that this presidential directive does not specify where these U.N. expeditionary actions are proposed to take place, whether in foreign countries or inside the borders of the United States. The globalists see no difference.

Two weeks after the release of PDD-13, the *New York Times* offered the comment that the directive was a turnabout from "long-standing tradition" which did not allow American soldiers to be commanded by foreign commanders, and added that, "the Clinton Administration is considering an expanded role in United Nations peacekeeping operations that would include having Americans serve under foreign commanders on a regular basis."

What is the ultimate significance of PDD-25? By the simple stroke of a pen internationalist Bill Clinton has opened the door wide for intervention within the U.S. by the U.N. And yet hardly a voice is raised in protest, except in those newspapers and books that the press characterizes as "neo-Nazi" or "right-wing extremist." G. Gordon Liddy's favorite epithet, "Ye suckers..." leaps to mind.

Another recent document of mind-blowing import is the working paper composed by the National Guard Bureau, dated June 24, 1994, titled "National Guard State Partnerships with the Russian Federation." Within this working paper President Clinton's "Bridge to America" scheme is detailed. The long and short of the plan is that "the National Guard Bureau has worked with the Joint [Chiefs of] Staff and the U.S. European Command to establish National Guard State Partnerships linking the National Guards of selected U.S. States with Ministries of Defense throughout Central and Eastern Europe (CEE) and Newly Independent States (NIS) of the former Soviet Union. These Partnerships seek to encourage long term institutional and people-to-people linkages and cement sustained relationships that can extend well beyond purely military matters."

"The Partnerships," the working paper continues, "assist the participating nations' transition to democratic military institutions with peacetime utility in providing military support of civilian authorities...

"The National Guard State Partnerships serve as a 'Bridge to America' to facilitate U.S. private sector involvement in this process. A promising relationship is developing at the national level between the National Guard Bureau and Sister Cities, International. State level cooperative efforts are underway with various organizations."

The paper goes on to reveal that over the past year and a half, National Guard State Partnerships have been approved with 14 ex-Soviet bloc countries. States which have already been hitched with foreign "partners" are California with the Ukraine, Colorado and Slovenia, Indiana and Slovakia, South Carolina and Albania, Utah and Belarus, Alabama and Romania, Illinois and Poland, Pennsylvania and Lithuania, Arizona and Kazakhstan, Michigan and Latvia, Ohio and Hungary, Maryland and Estonia, Texas and the Czech republic, and Tennessee and Bulgaria.

"The National Guard is anxious to extend the State Partnership Program to the Russian Federation. Now that the Russians have signed up for the Partnership for Peace, such an offer is both appropriate and timely. Such action would support the President's Partnership for Peace program and be an example of on-going bilateral success that could be emulated by our NATO allies.

"Russian acceptance would involve them directly with heartland America, the citizen-soldiers and airmen of the U.S. National Guard and Reserves and through them with the U.S. private sector. Conversely, such State Partnerships would serve to develop domestic U.S. support for the overall U.S. military outreach to the Russian Federation.

"Partnerships might be established... linking the National Guard of a U.S. State with a Russian Military District, a Russian Army Corps or other appropriate organization."

In other words, Poughkeepsie welcomes the Spetsnaz with open arms.

Related events of sheer idiocy (and idiocy has the ability to take on an amazing degree of sheerness these days) are covered in the story, "Crime Fighters Converge," published in *The New American* magazine for August 22, 1994:

"This July 4th, while millions of Americans were celebrating American independence, FBI Director Louis Freeh was in Moscow rhapsodizing over the growing interdependence between American and Russian law enforcement agencies. Freeh opened the FBI's first legal attaché office in Russia and joined Russian Interior Minister Viktor Yerin in signing a protocol which provides for close cooperation between the two agencies. 'We can honestly say that our two nations have more in common than ever before... We are united in purpose and in spirit,' declared Freeh in a Moscow press conference following the signing of the protocol. Sergei Stepashin, chief of Russia's Federal Counterintelligence Service (the successor organization to the KGB) was even more jubilant: 'Together, we're invincible.'

"The agreement was described by Freeh as a 'police-to-police bridge' between the two countries. Pursuant to the protocol, a hot line will be established between the FBI and the Russian Interior Ministry, and Russian police officers will undergo training at the FBI Academy in Quantico, Virginia."

Reports are coming out of the Soviet Union detailing a continuing commitment to bacteriological warfare operations and the construction of state-of-the-art military equipment (including the commissioning of four nuclear submarines this year), and the reorganization (but no diminishment in the size) of the KGB. Is it not even slightly possible that Russia is engaging the time-honored game of "playing possum"? One also notes the sudden rise of popularity of "hard-liners" and nationalists in Russia — could this be of possible long-term significance? These points, of course, may be rendered moot by the New World Order, and the surrender of the sovereignty of the United States to the communist-dominated U.N.

An interesting story was told by two Americans, John Younger and Bill Carlisle, who met two Russian women (one a former KGB agent, the other a former Russian police agent) at a rest stop near San Luis Obispo, California in October, 1993.

Younger, a Ukrainian American, was able to translate the Russian the women spoke. His account of the meeting was printed in the *Patriot Report.*

John Younger recalls, "I made a comment about the snow in Moscow in September. She commented, 'How can Americans be so gullible to believe what the news media is feeding them regarding the political and economic happenings in the world today? Their ability to control the weather is beyond your comprehension,' she told me. Luisa then commented, 'The planned starvation of the Ukrainian people will eliminate at least 20-30 thousand this winter alone.'

"Luisa told me that the people there are preparing in earnest for survival in the upcoming pre-planned campaign of genocide, planned by those in control of the country. Ukrainians are doing their best to accumulate livestock, plant gardens, store food, and do whatever else they can to prepare for the hardships that are to be intentionally visited upon them by their leaders.

"Luisa claimed to have been employed by the Secret Police there and was recently laid off as the primary task of preparing Ukrainians for subjugation by the coming New World Order has already been accomplished. Both women stated that they are employed at the Defense Language Institute in Monterey, California.

"'We are teaching an accelerated Russian language course to a ten-student class, 6 hours a day, 6 days a week.' Nina remarked there were currently over 100 teachers doing the same thing on a daily basis at the school, all with a similar background to hers.

"She made a most interesting comment that enlisted personnel have higher CIA status clearances than the officers do. She explained that the older officers still have too much allegiance to America to be fully trusted.

"Information flowed freely back and forth for some time. Interestingly, Nina continued to express surprise that all Americans weren't already cognizant of the future American-Russian joint plans to establish a police state here in Zone 10. (Zone 10 usually refers to Oregon, Washington and the Northwest states as they are sectioned off in the alleged plan to subjugate America. She clearly felt that Zone 10 included California.)

"Nina also appeared to be openly irritated with my American patriotism and commented, 'Why are you Ukrainians so stubborn and bullheaded to fight our inevitable world domination?' She added, 'We have so many of our agents working within your patriotic groups, using them to drive a wedge between people to prevent friendships from becoming lasting ones based on trust. We have been able to do this with fear and intimidation and it has worked perfectly in dividing the people and keeping them from uniting toward the common cause of freedom.'

"Without showing my anger, I told her about a recent gun show I attended where I saw tables of ammunition being bought out in a very short period of time, literally within an hour or two of the show's opening. 'Americans, like Ukrainians,' I told her, 'will not allow their country to be taken over and are waking up to the threat of the New World Order.' Nina retorted, 'We confiscated all registered weapons throughout the Soviet Union to prevent insurrections. Our new techniques of locating unregistered firearms have been perfected and may soon be put into use by your regulatory forces in America.'"

Give some second thought to whether the Russians are actually as dead a power as we have been led to believe, and while you're at it, you might even make some inquiries into the current status of Russian nuclear arsenals and the size of their standing army. Then take a look at the 'bridges' that the obvious socialist and possible Soviet agent Bill Clinton is building. Those bridges may begin to look like the planking needed to construct a Trojan horse.

It has been obvious that until recent years the United Nations has remained relatively ineffectual — and perhaps that image was even planned — but the power of this group has suddenly grown by leaps and bounds, according to the battle plan of the international controllers. The U.N. is intended to play a still-larger role in future international events, to the extent that it will be the international arbiter for world politics, and will possess an even more sizable standing army for enforcing its edicts.

A very interesting "Combat Arms Survey" was given to Marines stationed at the Twenty-Nine Palms Marine Base on May 10, 1994, and it has been all the talk in the conservative press of late. This survey was administered to Marines who had been involved in Operation Just Cause, Desert Storm, or Restore Hope, and offered an array of statements which the Marines were supposed to grade on a scale ranging from strongly disagree to strongly agree.

I have a copy of the survey, and here are some of the statements which were included:

"I would swear by the following code: I am a United Nations fighting person. I serve in the forces which maintain world peace and every nation's way of life. I am prepared to give my life in their defense."

"I feel there is no conflict between my oath of office and serving as a U.N. soldier. "I would be willing to volunteer for assignment to a U.S. combat unit under a U.N. commander."

"I feel the President of the United States has the authority to pass his responsibilities as commander in Chief to the U.N. Secretary-General. I would like U.N. member countries, including the U.S., to give the U.N. all the soldiers necessary to maintain world peace."

The last statement in the survey provides proof that the fictitious news release at the beginning of this book is based upon a real possibility which is currently being considered by the powers-that-be:

"The U.S. government declares a ban on the possession, sale, transportation, and transfer of all non-sporting firearms. A thirty (30) day amnesty period is permitted for these firearms to be turned over to the local authorities. At the end of this period, a number of citizen groups refuse to turn over their firearms. Consider the following statement: I would fire upon U.S. citizens who refuse or resist confiscation of firearms banned by the U.S. government."

A similar survey, according to the magazine *Modern Gun* (February 1994) was handed out to the U.S. Navy Seal Team Six in September of 1994. This survey posed the million dollar question in slightly different words: "Would you fire on U.S. citizens while in the process of confiscating their guns?"

Is a U.N. military invasion really planned for the United States? Although I have not been able to obtain independent verification of his statements, according to Mark Koernke, "The final level of military force which has just been structured this last year are U.N. Battle Groups inside the United States... Located on the northern border of California to Virginia will be the equivalent to a 34,000-man battle group. In the northern panhandle of Texas, near the Oklahoma fringe, will be (and is in fact) forming a 43,000-man battle group. Located in the Sacramento area is a 34,000-40,000-man force." Koernke believes that "22,000 United Nations troops are located south of Los Angeles" and that, "In addition to that, from Montana into the Canadian frontier, is a 37,000 man battle group" consisting of "two brigades E.E.C. mechanical infantry, two brigades Standard British Mechanized Infantry, the First Canadian Armored Division..." and "one light Japanese security brigade. Russian, Yugoslavian, Romanian and Korean U.N. troops are also being reported on U.S. soil by other reliable sources."

Koernke estimates the total number of forces confronting the American public as being "approximately equivalent to several heavy infantry divisions with a couple of mixed mechanized divisions combined. We are looking at a little over 300,000 personnel that we can verify or at least identify in different parts of the country." He notes forces located in Montana, Northern California, Southern California, Texas, North Carolina, Fort Drum, the Eastern seaboard and Washington, D.C. (with at least five units stationed there).

Is Koernke correct in his statements, or is he just a wild-eyed right-winger, seeing U.N. troops lurking behind every bush? I, frankly, am not certain. If he errs toward exaggeration, however, it is only in the matter of numbers. The U.N. has arrived, the New World Order has arrived, and freedom may soon be a thing of the past for the people of the United States.

8

The Crunch

Add it all up: the black choppers, the movements of war materiel and troops, the creation of "detention centers" around the country, the creation of a national police force which includes the capability of utilizing foreign troops, and finally Clinton's surrender of U.S. military authority to the U.N. (at least under "emergency" conditions). Even if only a small portion of these reports which we are receiving are true, the conclusion is inescapable: All of these activities are the preparations for a war which will be fought within the borders of the United States, a war planned to be initiated against the American people by the power hungry internationalists.

Hey, it's not like we didn't see it coming. Over the last fifty years America has been subject to a program of social control which has left it in a humanist, politically correct, multicultural, welfare-statist shambles. Since the institution of the Federal Reserve, income tax, the socialist programs of Franklin Roosevelt's mentor Colonel House, and the creation of the U.N. by the Council on Foreign Relations, we have seen gradual but killing incursions into the fabric of American life, and the destruction of the authority of the U.S. Constitution to the point where Bill Clinton and his masters now feel that it is possible to perform the coup de grace on freedom in America. Now the time is ripe to implement plans that will turn America into a socialist slave state in everything but name.

While the American public, by and large, concern themselves with such vital issues as whether O.J. Simpson is guilty of murder, and whether Michael Jackson's marriage to Lisa Marie Presley will somehow derail the investigation of his alleged child molestation, an alien invasion of the United States is taking place, and there are plans being implemented for the complete suspension of the Constitution, and for the total subjugation of America and its populace to an alien power, to alien armies, and to alien ideals.

For an insight into how the military, and the U.N. military, view people who might resist the New World Order, we may consult the *Sacramento Bee Final* for May 30, 1994. There is an article titled "Beware the Warrior Calls' — U.S. Unprepared for Emerging Threat, Pentagon Aide Says," the text which follows:

"An Army Major says in an influential military journal that the United States may lack the spine to fight its likeliest enemy. That enemy: a 'Warrior Class' rising around the world as traditional governments fall in places such as Haiti...

"In the new issue of *Parameters,* the journal of the Army War college, he writes: 'Unfortunately the enemies we are likely to face through the rest of this decade and beyond will not be soldiers,... but warriors — erratic primitives of shifting allegiances, habituated to violence, with no stake in civil order.'

"His article says the warriors spring from four pools:
1. The underclass, whose typical member he defines as 'a male who has no stake in peace, a loser with little education, no legal earning power...
2. Younger males shunted by the disruption of civil institutions into the underclass.
3. Genuine patriots, motivated by ideological belief or by personal loss.

4. Cashiered military men. They're the most dangerous... These men bring to other warriors the rudiments of the military art — just enough to inspire faith and encourage folly. The problem gets worse all the time... if the current trend toward national dissolution continues... by the end of the century there may be more of these warriors than soldiers in armies worthy of the name.

[First,] "To counter such 'warriors'... The army must shape up its intelligence gathering. While traditional intelligence crams facts into rigid geographic categories warriors roam. Second... Intelligence officers must set aside their preoccupation with numbers and weaponry. Instead... they must start reading books that explain human behavior and regional history. Finally... the Army must ask whether it can summon up the level of violence it needs.

"...This type of threat generally requires a two-track approach — an active campaign to win over the populace, coupled with irresistible violence directed against the warlord(s) and the warriors. You cannot bargain or compromise with warriors."

So listen, you post-NAFTA "erratic primitives," judging from the recent statements of the executive office and the controlled media, it must be apparent that the next step in the One World takeover of the United States will probably have to do with gun control. Guns, after all, were seen by the founders of this nation as a means for keeping government (and other tyrannical forces) off of the people's back. That hardly squares with the philosophy of the New World Order, which sees government as the answer to everything.

Here is the probable way that it is going to shake down. If there is any resistance to the disarming of the country by the populace, then the National Police Force (composed of the whole alphabet soup of government enforcement agencies, along with U.N. troops) will be mobilized through the declaration of a state of emergency. The justification for such an action might be spurred by an uprising of the people, something on the order of the takeover of the government which Waco-lawyer Linda Thompson proposed to have happen on September 19, 1994. Not to suggest that Thompson was dishonest in her assessment of what needs to be done to take back the country, I am simply saying that an action such of this could invite the kind of massive retaliation we are talking about.

The first targets of the martial law takeover of the United States will probably be gun owners — and this might be any gun at all. At the moment, legislation is in the congressional pipeline which would succeed in outlawing all guns, not just those of the "assault weapon" category. Along with the gun grab, one can expect a crackdown on various anti-authoritarian movements, such as the patriot movement, ethnic separatist groups of various colors, tax resisters, home schoolers, and people who are willing to stand up to or speak out against the totalitarian New World Order.

These are the groups and individuals who will be taken to detention centers (a.k.a. concentration camps). Cleaning out these "dissident elements" will leave the U.S. open for the final stage of the plan of the international controllers, which is really quite simple. By the year 2000 America will be merged into a Socialist New World Order, and the world will be split into three functional divisions: European, North American, and the Pacific Rim power structure. These international blocs will be governed by the United Nations, with the U.N. Army stepping in to quell any disturbances or "quaintly archaic" nationalist sentiments. The U.N. and allied New World Order lackeys such as Bill Clinton and George Bush are, despite all their humanist rhetorical debris, clearly the frontmen for the international bankers, "aristocracy," and world-spanning conglomerates who pull the strings from behind the scenes, and manipulate what takes place in this world through such elitist intermediaries as the Trilateral Commission, the Council on Foreign Relations, and the Bilderbergers. These are the groups who are bent on blowing away the sovereignty of all nations, and surrendering national controls into the control of a single governing body. Fewer guys to bribe that way.

Plans are now in full implementation for the surrender of U.S. sovereignty into the global New World Order, as envisioned by international banking and industrial controllers since at least the time of the formation of the Cecil Rhodes Round Table in 1891 (the group to which much of the One World maneuverings of this century can be traced). The real controllers of America are these invisible powers behind the scenes, supporting or shooting down succeeding presidential administrations. Virtually all of the members of presidential cabinets these days are members of these secretive groups who plan our lives from behind closed doors. These are the blue bloods and the frontmen of same, the types who have always drooled over the possibility of creating one big global plantation in which the vast majority of human beings labor long and are paid virtually nothing: this is the time-honored wet dream of the conspirators. And it is our New World Order nightmare.

Afterword

It is not a matter of conjecture anymore. The plan of the owners of the world is to institute a New World Order — in essence just the consolidation of world control into fewer hands. When the U.N. has a "peacekeeping" force superior to that of the U.S. military (or perhaps before that) there is no doubt, no argument, that U.N. forces will be used to subjugate the U.S. The forces who intend to implement the New World Order (and they include the politicians who currently rule the roost in the United States) simply will not take no for an answer.

There are only a few options for effective action that I can see (and I won't even call them solutions, since I am not certain that there is any time left for solutions). Here are a few of the possibilities which are open to you:

1. Be prepared for the worst. The internationalists are planning to turn America into one more colony on the global plantation, and any preparation you can make for self-sufficiency will at least buy you a little time when push comes to shove. Don't get the idea that you're going to live a happy life in the outback of Utah, though, while the New World Order goes on its merry way. Spy satellites now make that fairly unlikely. Better to stand up to the New World Order now — when we can at least speak out and vote — than run from it later.

2. Vote out of office any politicians who support the New World Order. Support politicians who will dismantle the New World Order conspiracy. Become a politician yourself, if you can play that game, or perhaps get next to one — get into their camp for access. If you can't play the political

game, then consider making up some fliers that expose some of the lackeys of Big Brother in your area. Get people talking. Get people screaming at the top of their lungs. Unfortunately, the prospects are slim for actually winning via the political route because the cards (and cash) are stacked in the favor of the politicians. They, after all, are simply a class of criminals who are unlikely to surrender control easily. If it looks like they are going to lose control of the government, then they are likely to initiate their endgame scenario of armed intervention. Still, this is one of our best possibilities for success at the moment.

3. Link up with and support pro-Constitutional, anti-New World Order groups in your area. Form a group and shock the hell out of the owners with a thousand advocates rallying on the lawn of the courthouse. Connect up with information sources which will give you accurate current news about what the New World Order is doing, and then pass that information along. Support any alternative movements that you believe will be effective in combatting the New World Order, be they political or non-.

4. If possible, home school your kids — it's a lot easier than it seems, and a month of home schooling will show you how little the public schools are doing. Why let your kids be indoctrinated with the government line?

5. Spread information on the New World Order totalitarian takeover to anyone you can, especially to politicians, people in the military, people in the media, and your Uncle Harry. Let thousands of people know what is happening to this country via fliers, computer bulletin boards, the Internet, radio talk shows, homegrown newspapers and newsletters, and public access television. Start a book and video store — even by mail-order — which will get the word out. This activity — spreading information on the New World Order conspiracy — is probably the most important of the op-

tions that I have listed, since we need many, many more individuals in our camp if we are to have even a slight chance of saving ourselves from complete tyranny. Go thee and multiply your viewpoint: spread information of the coming New World Order tyranny to everyone you can, and let them know that Big Brother is here to take away your guns first and then the last of your freedoms. Wouldn't it be excellent to see anti-New World Order book and video infomercials all over the TV dial instead of Regis and Butthead?

6. Use your own intelligence to evolve methods for stopping or, if worst comes to worst, overthrowing the New World Order.

7. Although the situation may be grimmer than grim, do not succumb to hysteria. We need to think clearly and to act clearly. Don't buy into every screwy scenario and bit of doomsaying that comes down the pike. Don't worry about aliens under the bedstead if the evidence shows it is the politicians who are going to do you in. Work to see through disinformation, even if it comes out of the mouth of a flag-draped "patriot." Do not set yourself up as a martyr like David Koresh and his followers, but take on the much harder task of communicating what people need to know and organizing to combat the forces who wish to further enslave us. I would especially encourage you to stay legal, so that you can carry on the fight rather than being shot down over some Rambo-esque grandstanding.

Now it is up to you. I do not advocate violence in any form — not that disclaimer is going to keep me off of a few choice lists once this book comes out. But I do advocate taking back this country and reforming it, by non-violent means, to restore freedom. The fact is, all I am suggesting is the protection of the current American constitutional system from the real subversive forces at work in this world. I urge you to do all you can to take this country out of the hands of the internationalist politicians and the bankers and the social controllers — and to stop the New World Order dead in its tracks.

Good luck, and keep me advised of your progress.

Sources

The Choppers ---- and the Choppers by Thomas Adams: Project Sigma, P.O. Box 1094, Paris, Texas 75461

The McAlvany Intelligence Advisor: P.O. Box 84904, Phoenix, AZ 85071

The Patriot Report: P.O. Box 122, Ponderay, Idaho, 83852

The Spotlight: 300 Independence Ave. SE., Washington, D.C. 20003

Recommended Contacts

A-Albionic Consulting & Research: P.O. Box 20273, Ferndale, Michigan 48220

Crash Collusion: P.O. Box 49233, Austin, TX 78765

Factsheet Five: P.O. Box 170099, San Francisco, CA 94117-0099

Flatland: P.O. Box 2420, Fort Bragg, CA 95437

IllumiNet Press: P.O. Box 2808, Lilburn, GA 30226

Leading Edge: P.O. Box 481-MU58, Yelm, WA 98597

Loompanics Unlimited: P.O. Box 1197, Port Townsend, WA 98368

Militia Of Montana: c/o P.O. Box 1486, Noxon, Montana 59853

Newspeak: 5 Steeple Street, Providence, RI 02903

Prevailing Winds Research: P.O. Box 23511, Santa Barbara, CA 93121.

Steamshovel Press: P.O. Box 23715, St. Louis, MO 63121

For a free copy
of our current catalog
write to:

IllumiNet Press
P.O. Box 2808
Lilburn, Georgia 30226